A One-Year Devotional
of 60-Second Warm-Ups

Hank Parker

www.xulonpress.com

ACKNOWLEDGEMENTS

For my Lord:

I am grateful to the Lord Jesus Christ, for His grace and help in being creative with the production of the "60-Second Warm-Ups."

For my family:

Thanks to my wife, Patsie, of 44 years who has stood faithfully by me in my walk of life. To our daughter, Christie Adams, who spent countless hours editing this book, and our daughter, Melanie Clark, who helped in the office in the early beginnings; I would like to say thanks for all your love and help.

For my friends:

Thank you, Shirley Huband, for your consistent faithfulness and dedication for years of airing the Warm-Ups daily by telephone; and being used by the Holy Spirit to bring this book to its original printing. To one of my best friends, David Jackson, from the radio field of expertise; thanks for inspiring me from day one, in the birthing process of the "60-Second Warm-Ups." I am grateful to Dean Patrick also, for being a true friend as well as a financial supporter of my ministry.

Also, my wife and I would like to thank George Walkey for his technical skills and for propelling the "Warm-Ups" back to a fresh new way of reaching many more who need a quick message in today's society, so we all can keep running the race for the Lord.

January 1

The Purifier

I am sure you know what an air purifier is. It takes air in, purifies it, and throws it back out as clean air. In James 1:22, the Bible says, "Be doers of the word and not hearers only, deceiving yourselves." When you know the Word, but don't do the Word, you're not purifying yourself. You have to take the Word in, let it filter and clean you by doing something with it. 2 Corinthians 2:15 says, "We are to God a fragrance of Christ among those who are being saved." Let the Word purify you so you can smell good to the sinner!

_____

_____

_____

_____

_____

January 2

Anger

Have you ever gotten angry? If you are human, you have. You probably said something you wished you hadn't said. The lawnmower didn't start; you kicked it and hurt your foot. Yes, I'm confessing before the brethren. Proverbs 16:32 says, "He who is slow to anger is better than the mighty, and he who rules his spirit than he who takes a city." That is a strong scripture. When the pressure is really on you, to be able to sing or quote a scripture is a good sign of maturity, but it doesn't come overnight. Thank God for the pressure, because it gives us the opportunity to show others by our actions that there is a Greater One living inside us

_____
_____
_____
_____
_____

January 3

Sheep Droppings

Have you ever left church and noticed bulletins, balled-up paper, and tissues scattered all over the seats and floor? I call those sheep droppings. The sheep come in and leave their droppings everywhere. In 1 Corinthians 6:19-20, the Bible says that your body is the temple of the Holy Spirit. You were bought with a price and glorify God in your body. Your body is not glorifying God by leaving trash behind when you leave church. So, glorify God everywhere you go, and watch out for the sheep droppings

_____

_____

_____

_____

_____

January 4

Squeezed Fruit

It takes a lot of time to grow good fruit. You need rain, sunshine, and fertilizer to bring forth good fruit in season. In Galatians 5:22, the Bible speaks of the need to bear forth good fruit, weaved all together, starting with love. Have you ever noticed that when you start bearing a little fruit, the devil sends someone to squeeze your fruit? Do you feel your fruit being squeezed? Verse 24 says in Christ we "have crucified the flesh with its passions and desires." If your fruit is being squeezed, that's okay – it's getting ripe!

January 5

Fools

Do you really know what the definition of a fool is? It is someone who lacks understanding or purpose. Have you ever acted foolish at times or know of someone who acts foolish? You tell them about the love of Jesus and the dangers of living in sin, and they pay no attention. Proverbs 14:9 says, "Fools mock at sin, but among the upright there is favor." If you are spending most of your time around fools, get away before that foolish spirit jumps on you. We need to fool-proof ourselves. They can't stab you in the backside - if you don't let them in the inside!

January 6

Attitude

Have you ever run into some people with an attitude problem? Maybe you have slipped into that area sometimes. When you got saved, you joined the body of Christ. You are a soldier of the King, a team that is working to build His Kingdom. In Philippians 2:2 the Bible says to be of one accord and one mind. When you have a bad attitude, the Lord puts you on the bench. You're still on the team, but you can't play because of your attitude. The anointing is not there to defeat the devil. Keep your attitude right, and you'll be victorious every time!

_____

_____

_____

_____

_____

January 7

At the Heart

It is so sad to hear Christians making prejudiced statements and favoring one another because of color. 1 Samuel 16:7 says, "Man looks at the outward appearance, but God looks at the heart." In Christ, there is no color, no male or female. We are one in the Body. When you see a black or white brother, you shouldn't look at color – that's the outward appearance; instead, look at the inside, at the fire of God. That will purify your stinking thinking!

_____
_____
_____
_____
_____

January 8

Aroma

Have you ever walked outside on a hot afternoon after taking a shower and putting on cologne and all of a sudden your aroma draws gnats and all kinds of bugs? In 2 Corinthians 2:15, the Bible says, "We are to God the fragrance of Christ among those who are being saved." As a Christian you have a spiritual fragrance, an aroma about you that draws sinners like flies. It's the anointing; some run away from it, but others are hanging around. Tell them where the fragrance came from - it's a heavenly cologne available to all that call on the name of the Lord!

_____

_____

_____

_____

_____

January 13

Flapping Wings

It is so awesome how God takes care of us; He is always on time. In 1 Kings 17:2-6, the Lord told Elijah to go to a brook in the Cherith Ravine, and that He had commanded the ravens to feed him there. Elijah would never have been fed by the ravens if he had not obeyed and went to the brook. Obey the Lord in what He tells you to do. The ravens could be referred to as the sinner whom you touched by doing what God told you to do. They want to bless you; are you ready? The wings are flapping - the blessings are coming!

January 14

Religion

Have you ever been talking to someone about Jesus, and they change the subject and start telling you about their denomination or church? They even throw in some Scriptures to make it sound good. In John 10:10, Jesus said, "I have come that they may have life, and that they may have it more abundantly." Religion pulls God down to their level; they try to get to God from the mind. Christianity is God coming to man through Jesus Christ. We change to God's image through the Bible. Christianity is a relationship with Jesus that brings freedom. Religion is a graveyard - nothing moves in a graveyard!

_____
_____
_____
_____
_____

January 15

Fat Hips

Have you noticed on TV and just about everywhere you go that people are talking about working out, dieting, and different types of exercises? I work out three days a week at the gym, and it is wonderful. It keeps the "roll" of the ministry off. 1 Timothy 4:8 says, "Bodily exercise profits a little, but godliness is profitable for all things..." Notice it says "a little". You need to take care of your temple so you can kick the devil every day, releasing the anointing in you. Be careful now, because a minute on the lips could mean a lifetime on the hips!

_____
_____
_____
_____
_____

January 16

Pray on Them

Have you ever gotten into a discussion with someone and it got a little heated? You walked away upset, knowing that you didn't handle that situation in the spirit; it was that old flesh out of control. You might be going about your daily routine and that person will come to your mind. The Lord is telling you to forgive. In Mark 11:25 Jesus said, "Whenever you pray, if you have anything against anyone, forgive him, so your Father may also forgive you." Pray it on them before you lay it on them. The Spirit was released, and the old flesh has died.

_____
_____
_____
_____
_____

January 17

Light Shine

I was talking to a friend the other day, who was talking about Christians struggling to stay hot for Jesus. In Matthew 5:16, Jesus said to let your light shine before men. He didn't say make your light shine, He said "Let your light shine." Before you were saved, you didn't make yourself curse; it came naturally; you didn't have to work at it. The devil flowed out of your life naturally. Now that you're born-again, let it flow out of your love for Him. It becomes fun and not work, because He's flowing through you!

_____
_____
_____
_____
_____

January 18

Stirred Up

There is a lot of pressure put on the church in these last days. The world wants to shake you from your foundation in Christ. In Hebrews 12:25, the Bible says, "See that you do not refuse Him who speaks." God wants to stir you, but not shake you. If you are listening to His voice, you can be stirred up in Him. If you walk away, you will feel the shaking of the world. Let Him stir you, so that when the shaking comes you will not be moved.

_____

_____

_____

_____

_____

January 19

Transparent

Just about everywhere you go, people are talking about racial problems. I can understand the world fighting over stuff like that, but not the church. In Galatians 3:28, the Bible says there is neither Jew nor Greek, slave or free, male or female; for you are all one in Christ Jesus. If you are looking at me in the spirit, you can't see my color. If you are saying what the Word says, then you are not speaking the flesh. Do you know what God's favorite color is? It's transparent - I like that color!

_____
_____
_____
_____
_____

January 20

God Called

Have you ever noticed some people come into the church and start bragging about their qualifications, abilities, education, money, etc.? What your position in life is means nothing to God. In 1 Corinthians 12:28, the Bible says that God appointed different ones in the church to do certain things. One of them is helps; the word "helps" means loving servant. If you start being a loving servant, the Lord will promote you. God does not call the qualified -
He qualifies the called.

_____

_____

_____

_____

_____

January 21

Resign to Resign

Have you ever stopped to think that in these last days, the devil wants to eat your lunch? He can't stand it when you are on fire for God. That's when you do him the greatest damage. The pressure is also the greatest, and when you get discouraged, that's when he moves in. In Ephesians 2:1, the Bible says, "And you He made alive, who were dead in trespasses and sins." Get up when you're knocked down; use your authority in Jesus" name. Don't resign to resign!

_____

_____

_____

_____

_____

January 22

Don't Lose Heart

Have you ever gotten discouraged in your prayer time and felt as if your prayers were not being answered? In Luke 18:1-8, Jesus said not to lose heart. He gave an example of a widow woman who went to an unjust judge; she was so persistent that the judge granted her request because of her persistence. Then Jesus said in verse eight, "...when the Son of Man comes, will He really find faith on the earth?" Keep thanking God for answering your prayers. Do not be weary-the answer is coming. It blesses Him so much when we are persistent in our faith; it blesses the devil when we fear and doubt. Let's bless the Lord with our faith.

_____

_____

_____

_____

_____

January 23

The Wills, Won't and Can't

Did you know that there are three kinds of people in the world? The Wills, Won'ts, and the Cant's. In Proverbs 6:2, the Bible says we are trapped by the words of our mouth. If you talk like you Will do it, it will get done. If you talk like you Won't, you will be against it. If you always say you Can't, you'll never do anything for Jesus. Get in the Will flow, and watch yourself go!

_____

_____

_____

_____

_____

January 24

Unbelievers

Have you ever been sharing Jesus with someone and they say they just don't believe the Bible or anything you are saying? John 20:31 says, "These (things) are written that you may believe that Jesus is the Christ (the Anointed One), the Son of God, and that believing you may have life in His name." In Psalm 55:15, the Bible says, "Let death grab them, let them go down alive into Hell..." They may be an unbeliever here on earth, but there are no unbelievers after death.

_____
_____
_____
_____
_____

January 25

Church

Have you taken the churches in your area for granted? I have, but not anymore. Did you ever stop to think what your town or city would be like if it weren't for those churches? In Ephesians 3:10, the Bible says, "To the intent that now the manifold wisdom of God might be made known by the church to the principalities and powers in the heavenly places." The word "manifold" means multicolored, a variety of shades. God expresses Himself in very different ways in the church. We need to thank Him for His many different expressions in the Body, to defeat the devil in your town!

January 26

Warfare

We hear a lot in the Body of Christ about spiritual warfare and how you can defeat the devil through prayer. That's good, but after prayer must come action. Why is the divorce rate 4% higher in the church than in the world? In James 2:20, the Bible says, "...faith without works is dead." What good is your "prayer life" without an "action life"? The world wants to see us in power, demonstrating the righteousness of God in public. You may preach what you know - but you will reproduce what you are.

January 27

Root for Fruit

Have you ever seen a picture of a tree and its root system? The bigger the tree, the stronger and deeper the roots. Each root is different, doing its job for the overall production of the fruit of the tree. In Romans 11:16, the Bible says, "If the dough offered as first fruits is holy, then the batch is also holy; and if the root is holy, so are the branches." God made you different than anyone else. Be yourself; develop good, deep roots in Christ. Thank Him for making you different and bloom where you are planted. The deeper the root - the greater the fruit!

_____

_____

_____

_____

_____

January 28

Stinking House

My wife was cooking some fish and the odors were really stinking up the house. I grabbed a can of disinfectant and went to work. In just a few minutes, the house was smelling sweet. Psalm 119:103 says, "How sweet are your words to my taste, sweeter than honey to my mouth." Speak the words of the Lord to your spouse and children; the atmosphere will be sweet-smelling with the aroma of heaven. The disinfectant didn't work until I pressed the button.
Push your button, and speak the words of the Lord.

_____

_____

_____

_____

_____

January 29

Telescope

Have you ever looked through a telescope? It will carry you a lot farther than your natural eye can see. In Romans 10:17, the Bible says, "Faith cometh by hearing, and hearing by the Word of God." Faith will carry you much farther than you can see, because you are looking with the eyes of the spirit and not the natural eye. When you speak the Word of God, your spiritual telescope reaches way out there and you can see it because the Word says so. Keep saying it, and it will come to pass. Use your heavenly telescope - it will bring things that are far away from you close!

_____
_____
_____
_____
_____

January 30

Religion

Have you ever been in a "religious" church? I mean a dead church, where nothing is happening. It's very hard to stay awake, and when you leave, you're exhausted. You wonder if you learned anything by going. In John 4:23, Jesus said, "...the true worshipers will worship the Father in spirit and truth..." The truth has to have spirit to be alive. Without the spirit, the truth is dead - it's religion. The bad thing about religion is they don't let the Holy Spirit do anything.

_____

_____

_____

_____

_____

January 31

Wax Bold

When I read the book of Acts, I am amazed at the boldness the early church had. It wasn't just the apostles; it was
everyone who went out preaching in the name of Jesus. In
Acts 13:46, the Bible says, "Then Paul and Barnabas waxed
[or grew] bold and said, „It was necessary that the Word of
God be spoken to you"…" Notice the word "wax" means to
grow. As we pray, read the Word, and witness for Jesus, we
are waxing bold for Him. Set your faith for the glory of God
to shine. Be diligent to wax bold - so you don't wax cold!

_____

_____

_____

_____

_____

February 1

The Belly

Just about everywhere you go, there are fast food places trying to lead us astray to future diseases. That's when our chest falls into our drawers. In 1 Timothy 4:8, the Bible says, "Bodily exercise profits a little, but godliness is profitable for all..." Notice it says exercise does profit a little. So let's hit the treadmill, pump that iron, and focus on good food for us - so we will not have the "roll" of the ministry.

February 6

Blessing

How would you like to be a continual blessing? It flows from a continual attitude. In Philippians 2:5, "Let this mind be in you which was also in Christ Jesus." Can you have the mind of Christ at all times? Yes, if you let His mind be in your mind. You will be a blessing wherever you go and to whomever you meet. Having a continual attitude of the mind of Christ will bring continual blessing. The world is so negative; the Church cannot allow this to slip into our way of thinking.

_____
_____
_____
_____
_____

February 7

Depressed Bird

I was sitting in my backyard one morning, drinking a cup of coffee and just enjoying the beautiful day, when I noticed these birds in a tree. They were singing and chirping, and acting like they didn't have a care in the world. The Lord spoke to my heart and said, "Have you ever seen a depressed bird?" All of the birds were happy. In Matthew 6:26 the Bible says, "Look at the birds of the air..." That's an example for us. We need to be like those birds - if God can take care of them, He can sure take care of us.

February 12

Idols

Have you ever noticed how many people are into idol worship, even Christians that love the Lord and go to church? This idol slips in very slowly and overtakes the Christian before they know what's going on. They actually think they are doing the will of God. In 2 Thessalonians 3:6-15, the Bible talks about people walking disorderly; that if they didn't work, they should not eat. They were busybodies causing problems in the church. They were into idol worship because they were idle. In verse 14, it says to share the word to help them, but if they do not listen, let them have their idol - because they are idle!

_____
_____
_____
_____
_____

February 13

Silver

It is such a blessing to see the Lord bringing the body of Christ together. It's exciting, but it can be painful at times. In Proverbs 25:4, the Bible says, "Take away the dross from silver, and it will go to the silversmith for jewelry." The dross is the impurities in the silver. In our flesh are a lot of impurities that have to be worked on- by prayer, the Word, church, and ministry. Heat causes the impurities to rise to the top of silver. Persecution that you receive daily for being a Christian will bring areas in your life to the surface. God didn't make any junk - let the world see that fine piece of jewelry that's been in the fire.

_____
_____
_____
_____
_____

February 14

Draw Near

I was talking to this guy one time and he said, "Hank, I lean on the Lord daily", but his life looked like he was leaning the other way. When other guys were cussing, he just leaned right in with the rest of them. When the Christians started talking about godly things, he just leaned right in with us. This brother could do some leaning! In Hebrews 10:22, the Bible says, "Draw near (or lean) with a true heart..." If you're leaning on Jesus, do it with a true heart, then you will not lean back when the heat is on!

_____

_____

_____

_____

_____

February 15

Season of Leaving

I was at a minister's meeting a while back and this fellow pastor told me that a sister in his church came to him and said, "Pastor, I am in the season of leaving." He was trying to help her on a problem that she was having, and she didn't want to hear it, so she got into the season of leaving. In John 15:2, Jesus says "...every branch that bears fruit He prunes..." Are you willing to be pruned for more fruit, or does the season of leaving want to hit you? In the season of leaving, there is no fruit, just a dead branch. Be careful of the season of leaving - it may have you grieving.

_____
_____
_____
_____
_____

February 16

Word is Sharp

I was watching an operation on TV one time and I noticed how skillful the surgeon was with his scalpel. In Hebrews 4:12, the Bible says, "The Word of God is living and powerful, and sharper than any two-edged sword..." A two-edged sword cuts both ways, but it is a clean cut. On the other hand, a hacksaw tears instead of cutting. In your conversation with people, do your words cut clean for a healing, or tear for destruction? "The letter can kill, but the Spirit gives life." Let the love flow, as the Word of God goes forth to cut clean. It will bring healing, and they will be out of the hospital in no time!

_____
_____
_____
_____
_____

February 17

Racism

I was listening to this brother one time who opened my eyes to racism. He said, "Racism is treating others as if they don't matter." The light came on in me. All of us at times have been racist. When you reject someone because of their color, you're saying, you don't matter. Are they Baptist or Pentecostal, Catholic or Episcopalian? In 1 Corinthians 13:5, the Bible says love never wants its own way and is not touchy. Let us draw near to Him so that we will treat others like they matter.

February 18

God's Power

I am sure all of you have walked into a dark room, looking for the light switch. When you found it there was relief, because the lights came on. Electricity is God's power in the natural; the Holy Spirit is God's power in the supernatural. In Matthew 5:16, Jesus said, "Let your light so shine before men..." Turn on that supernatural power to chase away darkness. The word "glory" means God's ways being exhibited in your life. Darkness will flee - because of Jesus in me!

_____
_____
_____
_____
_____

February 19

Wolves, Goats, and Sheep

Did you ever stop to realize that there are three types of people in the church - wolves, goats, and sheep? A wolf is sent by the devil to upset the unity of the church, but a good pastor will see it and run the wolf off. A goat on the other hand is different; he may want to butt heads with the pastor, but if he stays long enough, he'll turn into a good sheep. In John 10:27 Jesus said, "My sheep hear my voice..." If you confront a wolf, he'll take off. A goat will straighten up, after his head stops hurting. Sheep are such a blessing; they love the pasture they are in, and are content to bloom where God has planted them.

February 20

Missionary Dating

In 1 Peter 2:9, the Bible says we are a chosen generation, His own special people, that are called out of darkness into His marvelous light. Are you a single Christian dating someone who is not saved or who is walking in darkness? There is no missionary dating in Christianity. Oh, but Brother Hank, you don't understand; Jan's going to get him saved. There's no missionary dating. Find one that loves Jesus so much that you can see it in their talk and in their walk. Stay away from missionary dating!

_____

_____

_____

_____

_____

February 21

Faith Kite

Have you ever been going through a tough time and you just wonder, "Lord, what's happening, where are you in this situation?" In Hebrews 11:6 the Bible says, "Without faith it is impossible to please Him...and He is a rewarder of those who diligently seek Him." Faith is believing the problem is fixed, before it actually gets fixed. Faith says "I have the answer", before you really have the answer. Faith is being joyful when you feel like throwing in the towel. Faith is like a kite - the more contrary the wind, the higher the kite flies.

February 22

Talebearers

Calling all on-fire Christians that are praying and working hard in your church! Listen to this urgent message! They are hiding in the congregation, probably sitting right beside you - be on the look-out. They could pull you away and make you think you're doing the right thing. They are a menace to the move of God. They are like termites eating away at your home and you are not aware of it. Proverbs 26:20 says, "Where there is no wood, the fire goes out; and where there is no talebearer, strife ceases." Yes, these are talebearers spreading gossip and sowing discord. Apply a thick coat of the Word of God to them; as a result, they will repent, or the fragrance will run them off!

_____
_____
_____
_____
_____

February 23

Offended

I am just amazed these days at how touchy some people are. I am talking about Christians that say they love Jesus. In Matthew 24:10, Jesus said, "And many will be offended, will betray one another, and will hate one another." You can reach out and ask for forgiveness, but they always think they're right. Of course they have their scriptures to back them up, but it's all in their head. Get away from them. Love is not touchy; it remembers no wrongs, and it cannot hate. You may be a Christian, but you are not a doormat.

_____

_____

_____

_____

_____

February 24

On Fire

John Wesley was asked how he drew such big crowds. He said he set himself on fire, and the people came to watch him burn. Psalm 39:3, "My heart was hot within me; while I was meditating the fire burned. Then I spoke with my tongue." Have you set yourself on fire, so people can see you burn for the love of Jesus? Or has the devil been trying to cool you down? He can't if you don't let him. Set yourself on fire by reading the Bible and praying, and as you speak with your tongue, the fire will burn. Here comes the crowd!

———————————————————————————
———————————————————————————
———————————————————————————
———————————————————————————
———————————————————————————

February 25

Egotistical

Have you ever seen a person that has been eaten up with ego? They are egotistical big time. That's a person who is set on self, everything centers around them. Proverbs 29:23, "A man's pride will bring him low, but the humble in spirit will retain honor." The Lord's greatest work on earth was reducing a person's ego (self-centeredness). When a person no longer sees himself, then will the Son of Man be glorified. Oh, how we need to watch out for ego; it will show up when we least expect it. You may be asking yourself, "How can I recognize it when it shows up?" Look in the mirror - if you can see yourself, you're not crucified with Christ.

_____

_____

_____

_____

_____

February 26

God's Love

Have you ever stopped to think of how wonderful our Lord is? His love is so awesome. Read 1 Corinthians 13:4-8; this is God's nature, to love you no matter what you've done. It says love is patient and never rude or touchy. Love never remembers the wrongs you have done; love never wants its own way. When you are really in love with Jesus, you're happy. We are not judged by the number of times we've failed, but by the number of times we succeed. The number of times we succeed is in direct proportion to the number of times we can keep on trying. Keep on loving, and you'll keep on moving!

_____

_____

_____

_____

_____

February 27

Soul Talk

Have you ever caught yourself saying things like, "I think it ought to be this way," or "I want this at the mall," or "I feel like I want to leave"? That's soul talk. Your soul is made up of your mind, your will, and emotions. 3 John 2 says, "Beloved, I pray that you may prosper in all things and be in health, just as your soul prospers." Your soul needs the Word of God shot to it from your spirit every day so that it won't lead you astray. Your feelings can play tricks on you; your will can want too much, and your thinking can get too stinking - if it's not filled with good thoughts.

_____

_____

_____

_____

_____

February 28

Standing in Line

I was driving down the road one day and I noticed this long line that was standing outside the movie theater. I found out it was the latest movie out of Hollywood, and people were flocking to see it. There is coming a day when people will be standing in line to go to church; it is already starting to happen. In Luke 12:49 Jesus said, "I came to send fire on the earth..." The flames are starting to draw the crowds. The lines will start to form at your church; keep the flames hot with your prayers. They will come to watch the latest movie being provided by Heavenly Hollywood; the one having the leading role is not an actor, but the Creator Himself - Jesus Christ.

_____

_____
_____
_____
_____
_____

March 1

The Wrong Gate

I am sure you heard of the Heaven's Gate tragedy and how many people committed suicide following this cult leader. They were tricked by the devil into taking the wrong gate. Isaiah 14:9 says, "Hell from beneath is excited about you, to meet you at your coming." In Matthew 7:13, Jesus said, "Enter by the narrow gate; for wide is the gate... that leads to destruction." Going to Jesus is the only gate. If you are born-again, there is a Heaven's Gate that will be the true gate. Don't be tricked by the wrong gate - in Hell you're too late!

_____

_____

_____

_____

_____

March 2

Eating Words

Have you ever been around someone who is always putting their foot in their mouth? I've done it so many times that my breath smells like my feet. Proverbs 15:23 says, "A man has joy by the answer of his mouth, and a word spoken in due season, how good it is!" It is so wonderful to speak words that will edify and comfort. The anointing in you will rise up, and out will come the right word to change a person's life forever. Be careful to stay in the spirit; if you hold your tongue now, you won't have to eat your words later.

_____

_____
_____
_____
_____

March 3

Hated List

Have you ever noticed on TV, the F.B.I. will reveal those on their ten Most Wanted list? God has a seven Most Hated list, and it's found in Proverbs 6:16-19. There are six things that the Lord hates, and the seventh thing is an abomination to Him; that means it's detestable to Him. These six things are a proud look, lying tongue, hands that shed innocent blood, a heart that devises wicked plans, feet that are swift to do evil, and one who speaks lies. The seventh one is those who sow discord among the brethren- which is an abomination to God. If you are spreading gossip, you are working for the devil. Repent and pray for people; you don't want to be on God's Most Hated list!

_____
_____
_____
_____
_____

March 4

In Whom You Believe

I am convinced that the reason so many Christians are having difficulty in their lives is that they know the Lord as their Savior, but they know more about Him than they really know Him. 2 Timothy 1:12 says, "For I am not ashamed, for I know whom I have believed and am persuaded that He is able to keep what I have committed to Him..." That relationship keeps you from going astray; knowing Him makes you hungry for His Word. The Pharisees and the Sadducees knew about Him, but they were "sad you see" - because they didn't know Him.

_____
_____
_____
_____
_____

March 5

Zip the Lip

The Lord is really dealing with His people in these last days. The least little thing that we do outside the spirit, it seems we have to get it straight before we can go on. One area is the tongue, watching what we say about one another. In James 3:5, "The tongue is a little member and boasts great things. See how great a forest fire a little fire kindles!" When you speak in love, you're putting out fires; when you speak against your brother or spread his sin, you're setting fires. We can either zip our lip - or sink the ship!

_____

_____

_____

_____

_____

March 6

Hanging Together

It is so wonderful how the Lord is bringing the Body of Christ together. But some are having difficulty coming out of their comfort zone and learning how to love someone from another part of the body of Christ whom they are not used to fellowshipping with. In 1 Corinthians 13:9, the Bible says "We know in part..." The Lord is bringing the different parts together so we can learn how to love one another and appreciate each other's part. Are you being critical of the other parts? You might need that part one day; if we don't hang together - we will hang separately.

_____

_____

_____

_____

_____

March 7

Hell is Excited to Meet You

I was reading an article in a magazine the other day that said 80% of Americans consider themselves to be religious and believe in life after death. Most of them are looking for support, not salvation; help, rather than holiness. Isaiah 14:9 says that hell is excited to meet you at your coming. There are religious people going to hell every day, and when they arrive they will probably tell the devil, "I'm not supposed to be here. I'm a church member." Right now, make the devil mad - ask Jesus into your heart and receive that eternal life insurance policy!

_____
_____
_____
_____
_____

March 8

Wrong Number

I tried to call a friend of mine and I dialed the wrong number. The man who answered the phone sounded just like my friend. My friend had just returned from out of town, and I wanted to welcome him home. I said, "Welcome home, you mighty man of God!" This man started cussing at me on the phone. Well, this guy just pushed my button; the Holy Spirit rose up in me and I said, "Jesus loves you!" In Matthew 5:11-12 the Bible says, "Blessed are you when they persecute you, and say all kinds of evil things against you... Rejoice and be glad..." I believe I'll see that man in heaven one day - I'm so glad I got the wrong number.

_____
_____
_____
_____
_____

March 9

At the Mall

My daughter and I went to the mall the other day. We were just getting ready to walk in and these teenagers were cussing out loud, not ten feet from us. I said out loud "Melanie, Jesus is so wonderful, hallelujah! Jesus loves you guys; Jesus is so wonderful!" Those guys didn't know what to do. In James 2:19, the Bible says, "Even the demons believe and tremble." If the devil can go public, so can the Christian. Don't be intimidated by those devils; they are blinded, they can't see. Stand up for Jesus in public, it's so much fun. The blindfold will come off - when you turn Jesus loose!

_____
_____
_____
_____
_____

March 10

Feed our Faith

I read a quote one time that said, "We must feed our faith and starve our doubts." In Romans 10:17, the Bible says faith comes from hearing the word of God. Will you feed your faith and starve doubts by just saying the Word? In John 15:7, Jesus said, "If you abide in Me, and My words abide in you, you will ask what you desire..." Feeding our faith is not just knowing the Word, but spending time with the One who wrote the Word. It's out of your relationship that your confessing comes alive - starving your doubts and feeding your faith.

_____
_____
_____
_____
_____

March 11

Three Seasons

Did you know that in your life, there are only three seasons-receiving, serving, and giving? In our early days of being a Christian, we receive from those more mature in the faith, until we come to a time of serving and giving out what we have received. In serving, it keeps pride from coming in and swelling our heads from the things we have received and learned. The last phase of our life is giving. That's the time when we pass on to the next generation what we have gained; they need to start off where we have finished. In Psalm 63:8 the Bible says, "My soul follows close behind You..."
Enjoy receiving, serving, and giving!

_____
_____
_____
_____
_____

March 12

Coming to Church

I would like to ask the question, why do people warm their cars up on a cold morning? It is because of damage to the engine before the oil circulates. That's good enough reason. In Isaiah 10:27, the Bible says, "That his burden will be taken away from your shoulder... because of the anointing oil." If you just wake up, take a shower, get dressed, and come to church – you're still cold; the anointing oil hasn't circulated. You need to praise Him with singing and reading the Word. Get that anointing oil circulating so that at church time your valves won't be knocking. You won't miss a beat - you'll be warmed up to give the sacrifice of praise.

_____

_____

_____

_____

_____

March 13

Polished Shoes

My son-in-law and I were shining our shoes in the garage the other day, and he said, "Isn't it amazing how a little polish makes shoes look like new?" Isaiah 49:2 says, "He has made my mouth like a sharp sword...and made me a polished shaft." Do some areas in your life need to be polished, shined up to reflect the glory of God? Is your mouth sharp with the Word, to pierce the darkness and reveal the light? It won't hurt to put a couple of coats of polish on to shine brighter. It takes a little longer - but a spit shine is the ultimate shine!

_____
_____
_____
_____
_____

March 14

Hold On

Have you ever had one of those bad days where everything is going wrong? Well, count it all joy; the blessings are right around the corner. In Hebrews 10:22-23, the Bible says to "draw near with a true heart..." and to "hold fast the confession of our faith without wavering..." Notice we have to draw near with a pure heart. The trials will come, but hold on; the anointing is there to help you. That's a good sign that you're flowing in Jesus, when the devil is attacking. Look at Jesus, the Apostle Paul, and now you. Hold on, be strong - hold fast, and you will last.

March 15

Mercy

In Matthew 9:27 the Bible says, "When Jesus departed from there, two blind men followed Him, crying out and saying, „Son of David, have mercy on us!"'" In Vine's dictionary, it says mercy is the act of God; peace is the resulting experience. Jesus showed mercy; that released the power to heal the blind men. You want to get someone saved, show mercy; if someone needs healing, show mercy; if they are discouraged, show mercy. Release the act of God in your life, to bring peace to people the Lord brings your way. Love releases mercy - to penetrate darkness!

_____
_____
_____
_____
_____

March 16

Deer and Lion

Do you know how a lion can sneak up on a deer? When the deer hears something, he turns around to see what it is. The lion is so quick, he can stop and be still before the deer can look at him. After a while, the lion sneaks up on the deer, and he has his prey. In Romans 8:6, the Bible says, "To be carnally or fleshly minded is death, to be spiritually minded is life and peace." You can't defeat the devil with natural thinking; he will sneak up on you every time. We have to fight him with the Word of God, in the power of the Spirit, with the authority of Jesus Christ. So the next time you hear him sneaking up on you, if you're in the Spirit - you'll see him before he stops!

_____
_____
_____
_____
_____

March 17

Know-It-All

Have you ever gotten around people that think they know everything? They know the Bible, but when it comes to doing something, you can't find them or they have something to do. They are like a blister; they show up after the work is done. In James 2:26, the Bible says that faith without works is dead. People don't care how much you know - until they know how much you care.

_____

_____

_____

_____

_____

March 18

Untitled

Did you know that four thousand churches close their doors every year in America? The U.S. is the only country not keeping up with the population growth. In James 5:19-20, the Bible says "If anyone wanders from the truth, and someone turns him back... he would save a soul from death..." We need to go to the backslidden; there is still time for America. Let your light shine in public, people want to see it. They are hungry for someone to point the way - are you willing?

_____
_____
_____
_____
_____

March 19

Loafing

Have you ever noticed some people's reaction when you ask them to do something in the church? It seems they spend more time trying to get out of the job by griping, complaining, and giving dumb excuses. They have probably been like that all their lives. In Proverbs 22:6 the Bible says, "Train up a child in the way he should go, and when he is old he will not depart from it." You don't have to be "well-bred" to loaf.

_____

_____

_____

_____

_____

March 20

Fat Christian

I heard a brother say one time that he was a fat Christian. I said, "You're not fat, you're in good shape!" He said, "No brother, FAT stands for Faithful, Available, and Teachable." I said, "Right on, brother!" I want to be fatter tomorrow than I am today. In Ephesians 4:15, the Bible says, "Speaking the truth in love, we may grow up in all things into Him..." So desire to be a FAT Christian - Faithful, Available, and Teachable. Stay away from that worldly diet food and eat the rich word of God!

_____
_____
_____
_____
_____

March 21

Giving

It's so much fun giving to the Lord's work. In these last days, we are going to see a great outpouring of money into the church to help new converts coming in. In Proverbs 13:22, the Bible says, "The wealth of the wicked is laid up for the righteous." We will need the world's money for the Lord's work; but if you aren't a giver now, God won't trust you with it when it comes. Your heart has to be right. When it comes to giving, some Christians will stop at nothing.

_____
_____
_____
_____
_____

March 22

Marriage

It is so sad that so many marriages are breaking up. In 1 Peter 3:7, the Bible says, "Husbands, dwell with them with understanding, giving honor to the wife, as to the weaker vessel, and as being heirs together of the grace of life, that your prayers may not be hindered." Men, how can our prayers be answered if we are not honoring our wives? The Lord isn't impressed with my preaching on Sunday morning, if I am not honoring my wife during the week. If arguing would mean anything, some couples would have a perfect relationship!

_____

_____

_____

_____

_____

March 23

An Example

Have you ever been challenged with something and you want to be successful at it, but don't know where to begin? You look for the most successful person. When I started lifting weights six years ago, I looked for the biggest guy in the gym and got some pointers from him. Stay away from the doubters and complainers. In James 1:6, the Bible says, "Let him ask in faith, without doubting..." They are double-minded; Jesus was our best example of success. It hurts, but I've seen so many people fall by the wayside and say, "Christianity didn't work for me." Their eyes were on the wrong example.

_____

_____

_____

_____

_____

March 24

Psalm 91

Have you ever been in a tight situation, where bodily harm or your life has been in danger? The first thing that we think about in the natural is calling the police. In Psalm 91:11-12, the Bible says, "He shall give His angels charge over you, to keep you in all your ways. In their hands they shall bear you up..." Don't misunderstand- call the police if you have to, but use the name of Jesus to run the devil off. There is something about that Name; it brings all heaven to your assistance. So, when you're up against the wall, before calling 911 - call Psalm 91!

_____
_____
_____
_____
_____

March 25

Jewel

Christians express themselves in many different ways. In John 15:16, Jesus said that we should produce fruit. Sometimes we are like a pearl, there has to be irritation for us to shine. Sometimes we are like gold; we have to dig for the things of God to produce value in our lives. Sometimes we are like diamonds; when we are put under pressure, the beauty and power of God comes forth. Sometimes we slip, and become like a rock - it just lies there and does nothing.

_____

_____

_____

_____

_____

March 26

Microwave

Have you ever noticed a bag of popcorn in the microwave when you first put it in? Nothing happens for the first couple of minutes. Then all of a sudden- pop, and then another pop- and after awhile there is constant popping going on. In Galatians 6:9, the Bible says, "Let us not be weary in well-doing, for in due season we shall reap if we faint not." Keep praying and reading your Bible; stay out of strife, be faithful in church, and pray for your pastor. Let us stay in the Lord's microwave; He's not through with us. The Body of Christ is coming together - and there is some popping going on!

_____
_____
_____
_____
_____

March 27

Plans

Did you know that God has plans for you, and none of them include defeat? The devil also has plans for you, but all of them include defeat. Whoever we listen to determines the outcome of our lives. In 1 Thessalonians 5:24, the Bible says, "He who calls you is faithful, who also will do it." He's called you to do something for Him. Proverbs 19:20 says, "Listen to counsel and receive instruction, that you may be wise in your latter days." A builder builds a house by the blueprints. The Lord has a plan for you - stay in the Bible, and it will come to pass.

_____

_____

_____

_____

_____

March 28

Dancing

I was talking to someone a while back who asked me if we dance in church. I said, "Sure!" In Psalm 149:3, the Bible says, "Let them praise His name with the dance..." When you get up in the morning, start praising the Lord and dancing before Him. The joy of the Lord is your strength. Exercising is stressed a lot these days; the best way to stay in shape is dancing unto the Lord. A man asked me one time if I stopped dancing when I got saved; I said "No, I just changed partners!"

_____

_____

_____

_____

_____

March 29

Opportunity

Have you ever been around some Christians that know the Bible? They will quote you verses at the drop of a hat, but they never seem to accomplish much in life. In James 2:17, the Bible says, "That faith by itself, if it does not have works, is dead." It's good to know what the Bible says, because your faith is built on the knowledge of the Word. But the reason opportunity passes some people by is because they don't want to take advantage of hard work.

_____

_____

_____

_____

_____

March 30

Degrees

Have you ever been around some people who like to talk about the educational degrees they received? Don't misunderstand, I think it's wonderful to receive as much education as you can; but some people just like tooting their own horn. In Psalm 147:6, the Bible says, "The Lord lifts up the humble..." Walking in humility and love will always bring you before the right people at the right time for the blessings of the Lord to flow. The next time you are around someone when they're talking about their degrees, tell them you have two degrees: a B.A. and a D.D. – Born-Again, Devil-Destroyer!

_____
_____
_____
_____
_____

March 31

Negative

I am sure you have read your Bible, and noticed how positive Jesus was in His words and actions. There wasn't a negative bone in His body. He charged the atmosphere with the glory of God wherever He went. In Psalm 119:103 and 105, the Bible says, "How sweet are Your words to my taste, sweeter than honey to my mouth. Your Word is a lamp to my feet and a light to my path." The more we taste Him, the brighter our path gets. The light is on our feet, to direct our path on what we do. Negativity will exist as long as positive people do nothing.

_____

_____

_____

_____

_____

April 1

Falling Forward

It's so sad, but I am running into a lot of Christians who are dwelling on the past and not walking in the joy and victory that Christ paid the price for. I am convinced it's a lack of understanding regarding the new creation. In 2 Corinthians 5:17, the Bible says if any man be in Christ, that word Christ means anointed, he is a new creature. The old has passed away, and all is become new. Dwell on the new man in you; the old man is dead. Talk to the new man. You may have missed it, who hasn't? There is no sadness in failure - as long as you fall forward!

_____

_____

_____

_____

_____

April 2

Pushers and Hookers

You know, we hear a lot about pushers and hookers. The drug pusher tries to push drugs on our kids; they mess up people's lives for years and even lifetimes. A hooker is a prostitute who hooks men into sin, pulling them away from their wives and destroying their families. In Proverbs 5:1, the Bible says for us to pay attention to wisdom and listen to understanding. The Word of God keeps us on track. If you are a Christian, you can be a pusher and a hooker, too - we push the Word of God, and then we hook them into Jesus!

_____
_____
_____
_____
_____

April 3

Head Bypass

I'm sure you have heard of a family member or friend, who has had a heart bypass. So many times, we as Christians need a head bypass. Our heads get clogged up, trying to figure everything out instead of receiving by faith. Faith doesn't think, it acts. Faith comes from the heart, not the head. In Mark 11:23, Jesus said, "Whoever says to this mountain, „Be removed and be cast into the sea, "and does not doubt in his heart, but believes that those things he says will be done, he will have whatever he says." You build faith by reading, believing, saying, and then doing what the Bible says. Stop trying to figure it out, you're not that smart. Receive your head bypass from the Lord - and start having fun, living by faith.

April 4

Prayer Week

I'm so happy to hear that the body of Christ is starting to pray like never before. Everywhere I go, I hear about people having prayer meetings for revival in that area. Reports are being shared about revival coming down because of prayer; the whole community starts to change because of prayer. In 1 Timothy 2:1-2, the Bible says that prayers should be given for all men in authority, that we might lead quiet and peaceable lives. Is your community quiet and peaceable? Let's get to praying - one week without prayer makes one weak!

_____

_____

_____

_____

_____

April 5

Set Free

Have you ever stopped to think that the truth will not set you free? Just because you go to church and have a Bible in your hand, that doesn't make you free. You could have a stack of Bibles at home, but you're still not free. In John 8:32, Jesus said, "You shall know the truth, and the truth will set you free." You have to know the truth to be set free. When you ask Jesus to forgive you and He comes into your heart, you are free. As you read the Bible as the truth, you are set free. The more you read, the freer you become. If your Bible has dust on it, you're not free. Open it up and freedom will come.

_____
_____
_____
_____
_____

April 6

Faith or Fear

As Christians, we are supposed to be people of faith, but at times it's real easy to slip into fear if we are not careful. Faith believes what you cannot see will come to pass; fear is also believing what you cannot see will come to pass. Faith will lead to victory, but fear will lead to defeat. Which one will you choose? In Romans 10:17, the Bible says, "Faith comes by hearing, and hearing by the Word of God." The Bible also says God does not give us a spirit of fear. Tell the devil what God says, not what you think; he'll laugh at what you think, but run at what God says!

_____

_____

_____

_____

_____

April 7

Pharisee

It amazes me sometimes at the things Christians can complain about. A new convert gets on fire and the complainers, doubters, and religious people gather around him and fill him with everything but the things that can help him grow. In John 6:41, the Bible says that the Jews complained about Him because He said, "I am the bread which comes down from heaven." When that bread touches a new convert, there is a wildfire in the air, and we don't need a bunch of wet blankets trying to put the fire out. Are you on fire - or are you a wet blanket?

_____
_____
_____
_____
_____

April 8

New Book

A friend of mine told me of this new convert who went into the Christian bookstore and wanted a Bible. The lady asked him did he want the Old or the New Testament. He said, "Lady, I am paying good money- I want a new book!" Aren't new converts precious? In Matthew 5:8, Jesus said, "Blessed are the pure in heart, for they shall see God." Isn't it wonderful that He looks at our hearts and not at what we know? Let's stay in that "first love" state - and we will not faint!

_____
_____
_____
_____
_____

April 9

Felt like Quitting

Have you ever felt like quitting? You love Jesus with all your heart, but because of so much immorality, drugs, and violence, people seem to be coming at you for no reason. Well, hang in there, Church, there is good news. Hebrews 10:22-23 says, "Let us draw near with a true heart in full assurance of faith, having our hearts sprinkled from an evil conscience and our bodies washed with pure water. Let us hold fast the confession of our hope without wavering, for He who promised is faithful." If you haven't quit, you're winning. Stay in there and fight the good fight of faith. Remember the devil has no teeth - just loud barks.

_____
_____
_____
_____
_____

April 10

Joy is Full

I was at the gas station the other day filling up my tank and wasn't paying much attention to what I was doing, and ran the gas over the top onto my hand; it was full. John 15:11 says, "These things I have spoken to you, that My joy may remain in you, and that your joy may be full." We need to stay full of joy; let your joy run over to someone like that gas did on my hand. Keep your heart right, pray in the spirit and with your mind; read the heavenly newspaper each day to stay full. One thing was true about that gas tank - I couldn't get anything else in it. If you stay full of joy, there is no room for the devil!

_____
_____
_____
_____
_____

April 11

Working Hard

Have you noticed lately that many people are working hard to go to hell? Just look around you, most of them do not have time when you share Jesus. They are in such a hurry to get away from you; they just don't want to face the music. In 2 Peter 3:10-11, the Bible says, "The day of the Lord will come as a thief in the night...and the elements will melt with fervent heat; both the earth and the works that are in it will be burned up. Therefore, since all these things will be dissolved, what manner of persons ought you to be in holy conduct and godliness"? Don't give up, saints, hang in there. Keep the fires of Jesus burning in your heart; our King is coming soon. The world is depending on us - we are all they have to show for Jesus.

_____
_____
_____
_____
_____

April 12

Gripers

Have you ever been around some people that love to gripe? They say, "Why isn't the church doing this, and why aren't they doing that?" When the local church starts a building program, they are the first to gripe. When the young people want to do something, here comes the gripers, but they never volunteer to help. They are always there to give their two cents worth, but never their talents. In Isaiah 58:9-10, the Bible says, "...If you take away the yoke from your midst, the pointing of the finger, and speaking wickedness, then your light shall dawn in the darkness..." Have you ever noticed that the givers never gripe- and the gripers never give?

_____

_____

_____

_____

_____

April 13

Pressure

Have you ever been to a junkyard and seen those wrecked cars crushed into a little box? Maybe you've seen it on TV or at the movies. In 2 Timothy 3:12-13, the Bible says, "... all who desire to live godly in Christ Jesus will suffer persecution. But evil men and impostors will grow worse and worse, deceiving and being deceived." Yes, the devil wants to crush us and destroy our light. Psalm 37:12-13 says, "The wicked plots against the just, and gnashes at him with his teeth. The Lord laughs at him, for He sees that his day is coming." When the pressure is on, share Jesus and the devils will back up. They will try to put you in their crusher, but laugh at them in the joy of the Lord!

_____
_____
_____
_____
_____

April 14

Call on Jesus

It is so easy for us sometimes as Christians, when having difficulties such as sickness, to call our doctor first. That's the first thing the world does. Now don't misunderstand me; I praise the Lord for doctors and the many accomplishments they have made; we have a family doctor ourselves. However, I believe we as believers should go to the Lord our Healer first, and apply our faith in that area. If we need assistance from a doctor, don't get under condemnation. Go to him; the Lord can work through him, too. In Hebrews 11:6, the Bible says without faith it is impossible to please God. So the next time you have a headache, take two prayers and call on Jesus - before you go to the medicine cabinet.

April 15

Doubt

It is so amazing how I find myself saying things that I shouldn't say. In Mark 11:23, Jesus said, "Whoever says to this mountain, „Be removed and cast into the sea," and does not doubt in his heart, but believes those things he says... he will have whatever he says." Our mouth needs to line up with the Word and speak to the mountain. If we are speaking the problem all the time, the mountain gets bigger. The next time the devil hits you with doubt, just say, "I doubt that!"

_____
_____
_____
_____
_____

April 16

Knives, Forks, and Spoons

Have you ever taken notice of your knife, fork, and spoon at the dinner table? Your knife cuts the food, your fork stabs the food, and the spoon lifts the food. In Colossians 4:6, the Bible says, "Let your speech be with grace, seasoned with salt, that ye may know how ye ought to answer every one." Are your words stabbing people like a fork or cutting people like a knife? Let's lift them up like a spoon - with the words of grace coming under them, bringing them up higher in Christ. I like the spoon a lot better than the knife or fork!

_____
_____
_____
_____
_____

April 17

Measuring the Heart

Have you ever gone into a clothing store to buy a pair of trousers? The first thing the salesman does is measure your waist to see what size you need. You could have a nice-looking pair of trousers, but if they are too big, they would fall off while walking and that would be embarrassing. In Matthew 5:8, Jesus said, "Blessed are the pure in heart..." When God measures something in our lives, He always puts the tape measure around our heart. You don't want to be embarrassed in public!

_____
_____
_____
_____
_____

April 18

Circumstances

Have you ever asked someone how they are doing and they say, "Fine, under the circumstances." That word circumstance is actually two words brought together - circle and stand. In Ephesians 6:13, the Bible says, "Therefore take up the whole armor of God, that you may be able to withstand in the evil day, and having done all, to stand." How are you standing in your circle of circumstances? Let's be on top - and not under.

April 19

Vision

Have you ever thought that God does have a vision for us? But Satan also has a vision for us. In John 10:10, Jesus said, "The thief does not come except to steal, and to kill, and to destroy. I have come that they may have life, and...have it more abundantly." Yes, the devil has a vision and that vision is to kill and destroy areas of your life. But God's got a vision, too, one of salvation, health, and happiness. Come on, jump on the life train - it's coming by! Do you hear that heavenly whistle blowing?

_____

_____

_____

_____

_____

April 20

Thoughts

We have often heard teaching on avoiding strife with one another. Strife means bitter struggling and contention. Did you ever stop to realize that you could be in strife with yourself? In James 1:4, the Bible says, "Let patience have its perfect work..." Patience is a fruit of the spirit that is grown and developed out of trials. If you are in strife, struggling to make something happen rather than waiting on God, the fruit of patience can't come forth. When you argue with yourself, you never win.

_____

_____

_____

_____

_____

April 21

Undertow

I was watching TV the other day, and they were talking on the dangers of undertow at the beach. If a swimmer gets caught in an undertow and he doesn't break loose, it keeps him under and carries him out to sea. In Hebrews 10:23, the Bible says, "Let us hold fast the confession of our hope without wavering, for He who promised is faithful." The devil wants to keep you under and carry you away from the Lord. Hold fast and do not waver - victory is on the way!

_____
_____
_____
_____
_____

April 22

Meditation not Beditation

Have you ever waked up in the morning, and felt like you wanted to sleep a little longer- like two or three hours longer? While you are lying there, about to yield to your flesh and go back to sleep, your spirit speaks to you and says, "Start praising the Lord. Get up from there and read your Bible, sing and make a joyful noise so you can give the devil a hard time today." In Proverbs 6:9, the Bible says, "How long will you lie down, O sluggard? When will you arise from your sleep?" Train yourself more in the area of meditation -rather than "beditation."

_____
_____
_____
_____
_____

April 23

Three Voices

Did you know that you have three voices on the inside of you? Sometimes all three are speaking at the same time. We have to know which one to listen to or we might make a wrong decision that we will regret later. In Proverbs 20:27, the Bible says, "The spirit of man is the candle of the Lord, searching all the inward parts of the belly." Your conscience is the voice of your spirit; your reasoning is the voice of your mind, or soul; your feelings are the voice of your body. Feed yourself on the Word of God, and pray often. Let that candle in your spirit speak to those other two voices and tell them who is boss!

_____
_____
_____
_____
_____

April 24

Weed Killer

Have you ever had weeds coming up through your driveway and every year you have to put the weed killer down to kill them? If you don't, it will get worse. In 1 Timothy 2:8, the Bible says, "I desire therefore that the men pray everywhere, lifting up holy hands, without wrath and doubting (or dissension)." Come up in your life. Those weeds did not leave until I applied the weed killer; anger and dissension will not leave unless you pray and seek His face. Apply the heavenly weed killer - it works on everything.

_____
_____
_____
_____
_____

April 25

False Teachers

Have you ever been walking through the woods and brushed against some poison ivy? You never even noticed it, because it blended in with the other plants in the woods so well. After a while, when you started breaking out, you realized what happened. In 1 Timothy 4:1, the Bible says, "Now the Spirit expressly says that in latter times some will depart from the faith, paying attention to deceiving spirits and doctrines of demons." Do you know how you can tell if a false teacher is around? They never want to witness for Jesus to get people born again. If you hang around them long, you won't witness for Jesus either; that false doctrine will give you poison ivy. Listen to the Holy Spirit - He'll show you where the poison ivy is!

_____
_____
_____
_____
_____

April 26

Right Number

My daughter Melanie and her friend Elizabeth were at the mall one day and some boys came up wanting their phone numbers. Realizing they were not getting anywhere, they left. When they told me, I said they should have given them their numbers: John 3:16, Romans 3:23, Romans 6:23, Romans 10:9-10, and Romans 10:17. If they would have dialed all those numbers, heaven would have answered and said, "Salvation has come unto you." We Christians have so many opportunities to put the devil on the spot. I am not ashamed of the gospel of Jesus Christ, for it is the power of God unto salvation. They want to call - let's be ready with the numbers!

_____
_____
_____
_____
_____

April 27

Be Quiet

I recently had surgery on my throat, and the doctor said I couldn't talk for ten days. I thought, Lord, how am I going to do that? I had always been a talker; my wife thought I talked too much sometimes. Well, during those ten days the Lord taught me a lot. I learned to listen with greater detail. I would have to think more about situations before acting on them. It was hard, but wonderful. Maybe some of you need to talk more, but for me, it was learning how to tame the tongue. In Colossians 4:6, the Bible says, "Let your speech always be with grace, seasoned with salt, that you may know how you ought to answer each one." Try going a day or so without talking - it will sure help your listening.

_____
_____
_____
_____
_____

April 28

Forgive Quick

A friend of mine got a splinter in his hand. He didn't think that much about it, but in a few days it started to swell and turn red. He went to the doctor, who told him if he had let this go unattended, his finger would really have been in danger. That's how infections work, it keeps on spreading. In Mark 11:25, Jesus said when you stand praying, forgive. Let's be quick to forgive, so the healing process of God can keep the infection from spreading; it's all up to us. If my friend had not gone to the doctor, he wouldn't have gotten better. Let's go to the heavenly doctor - confess to Him, and watch the healing begin!

_____
_____
_____
_____
_____

April 29

Radiator Leak

I had some trouble with my radiator; it had a small leak, and I had to put water in it about once a week. Well, I took it to a man that fixes radiators; he said he could fix that one, so I wouldn't have to buy a new one. I went back the next day to pick it up. He said under pressure, it worked fine; it was all painted and looked like new. I took it home, put it in the car, added some water and antifreeze, and put the cap on. A few days later, it was leaking again in the same place; it didn't leak until it was under pressure. In 1 Timothy 4:1, the Bible says, "In the latter days some will depart from the faith, giving heed to seducing spirits, and doctrines of devils." Be careful; just because it's painted and looks new is no sign it's of God, until the pressure is applied.

April 30

Have it Your Way

I was talking to a brother the other day about a situation he was going through. I showed him in the Bible what it said about his situation. He said, "I don't care what anybody says, I'm going to do it my way." In Isaiah 55:8, the Bible says, "For My thoughts are not your thoughts, nor are your ways My ways." You may ask, "Well, how can I tell?" Are your ways going by the Bible? Does it lift up Jesus, or yourself? Will your way help other people, or hurt? Watch out for self, this isn't about having it your own way; it's Jesus - and we have to have it His way!

_____
_____
_____
_____
_____

May 1

Taking More Land

Have you ever felt like sitting back and taking it easy for a while? You are sharing your faith daily, standing up against the devil when he sticks his head up. You've been a good soldier, but you're tired; your mind tells you that you need a break. In Joshua 13:1, the Lord said to Joshua that he had grown old and far in years, but there is very much land that needs to be possessed. Joshua and his army had defeated thirty-one kings, but the Lord said, "You haven't finished yet." The devil wants us to lay back, because we're gaining ground. Tell people about Jesus every day - stand up for what the Bible says. When you do this, you are taking more land for the Kingdom of God.

May 2

Good God

We have such a good God; He loves us so much, and He wants us to tell Him we love Him. In Psalm 34:8, the Bible says, "Good and upright is the Lord..." In Psalm 34:8, it says, "Oh, taste and see that the Lord is good..." When you read His word, you are tasting goodness. We have a great God. Like my daughter says, "He is awesome, Daddy." Psalm 103:11 says, "For as the heavens are high above the earth, so great is His mercy toward those who fear Him." Tell Him you love Him every day; call Him a good and great God. He will fight your battles for you if you praise His name. God is good, God is great - I'm so glad I got saved, before it was too late!

_____
_____
_____
_____
_____

May 3

Keep the Lid off the Jar

Did you know that you can put fleas in a jar, and they will jump out as soon as you put them in? If you put a lid on that jar, come back later and take the lid off, they will not jump any higher than the top of the jar; they'll stay in the jar. God's Word, picked apart and taught with doubt and fear, will keep you in bondage. In Romans 10:17, the Bible says, "Faith comes by hearing, and hearing by the word of God." When you believe what that book says and act on it, your faith is built up, and before long, you're jumping out of the jar. Stay away from people that tell you to stay in the jar; if you continue to doubt, you'll hit your head on the lid every time.

_____
_____
_____
_____
_____

May 4

Keep Believing

I just can't understand why we as Christians can't believe the Bible for what it says. If God said it, why can't we believe it instead of trying to figure it out? In 2 Corinthians 11:3, Paul said, "But I fear, lest somehow, as the serpent deceived Eve by his craftiness, so your minds may be corrupted from the simplicity that is in Christ." If someone tells you that miracles were done away with when the apostles died, then you know they have been deceived. If people are getting saved today (and we know they are), then people are getting healed and demons are being cast out. The Bible is so simple - you would need somebody to help you misunderstand it!

May 5

What You Think You Are

Have you noticed lately how the world reacts when you tell them you're a Christian, especially when they see you living like one? They will try everything they can to get you to compromise with them, so that they won't feel convicted for the way they live. They want to make you feel guilty for being a Christian. We need to make them feel guilty for being a sinner, by showing love and talking what the Bible says. In Philippians 3:3, Paul says, "...Have no confidence in the flesh." You have to believe that you are more powerful than the devil, and act like it. Remember, it's not what you are that stops you – it's what you think you're not.

May 6

You are Appointed

I was talking to a man who was appointed to a high office in his company. In John 15:16, Jesus said, "You did not choose Me, but I chose you and appointed you that you should go and bear fruit, and that your fruit should remain." My friend was appointed because of the good job he did. Jesus did all the work at Calvary, and when we put our trust in the blood that was shed for us, we were appointed to preach the good news to the world. 2 Corinthians 1:21-22 says He has anointed us in God, sealed us, and given us the spirit in our hearts as a deposit. So you just remember that you are not only appointed, but you are anointed!

_____
_____
_____
_____
_____

May 7

Calling

Do you know what God called you to do? God works out of the local church, so stay in your local church to develop your calling. In Habakkuk 2:2-3, the Lord said, "Write the vision and make it plain on tablets, that he may run who reads it. For the vision is yet for an appointed time; but at the end it will speak, and it will not lie. Though it delays, wait for it..." Do not be anxious to develop your calling; it will come in due time. Serve in the local church and the Lord will exalt you in due time. He sees what you are doing and He will reward you openly when you serve in secret. You don't want to jump out too soon - the devil loves it when we are out of God's will.

_____
_____
_____
_____
_____

May 8

April Showers

April showers bring May flowers; when it rains in April, here come the flowers in May. In Isaiah 30:23, the Bible says, "He will give the rain for your seed which you sow in the ground." Rain cannot do anything for a seed unless we sow it. May flowers can't come forth from April showers unless there are seeds in the ground. The Bible says we are the sowers; when you open your mouth about Jesus Christ, that's a seed going into someone. When you continue to pray for them, your prayers are the rain. The more you pray, the more it rains on that seed. Just like the May flowers burst forth from April showers - so a new Christian will come forth from your seed!

_____

_____

_____

_____

_____

May 9

Sour Pickle

The other day my family and I were eating lunch, and I just love dill pickles. But when I opened the jar and took a bite, it was so sour, my mouth and face wrinkled up. My wife had made a mistake, and bought sour instead of dill pickles. If we are not careful, the world can see us as wrinkled-up, sour Christians. In Psalm 16:11, the Bible says, "In thy presence is fullness of joy..." Let's let the world see the joy of the Lord on our face - not an old, sour pickle.

_____
_____
_____
_____
_____

May 10

Retirement

A lot of people are talking about retirement these days. They say, "Can't wait till I retire. I'll just sit back and do nothing." As Christians in the army of God, there is no retirement. In 2 Timothy 4:7, the apostle Paul says, "I have fought the good fight, I have finished the race, I have kept the faith." There is no retirement in God's army. Jesus said in Matthew 5:10, "Blessed are they which are persecuted for righteousness" sake." When someone gives you a hard time because you are a Christian, don't think about retirement. Count it all joy to be persecuted for Christ, and then when He takes you home, He'll give you your retirement crown!

_____

_____

_____

_____

_____

May 11

On Trial

If you were put on trial for being a Christian, do you think there would be enough evidence to convict you? 1 John 2:4 in the Living Bible says, "Someone may say, I'm a Christian, I'm on my way to heaven, I belong to Christ." But if he doesn't do what Christ tells him to, he is a liar. What is Jesus telling us to do? Matthew 5:16 says let your light shine before men. Tell them about the love of Jesus with your mouth, and live what you are saying, so there will be enough evidence to convict you - if you're accused of being a Christian.

_____
_____
_____
_____
_____

May 12

The Stamp

When you send a letter in the mail, the Post Office will not mail it unless it has a stamp on the letter. When you became a Christian, the Holy Spirit put the stamp on your letter and said, "I will send you to places that will set people free." When God looks at you, He sees Jesus His Son who was sacrificed for you, and He is your postage stamp to go where God wants you to go. In Isaiah 6:8, the prophet said, "... Here am I, send me." Let's all be willing to jump into God's mailbox, because the stamp of approval is already there, to go to the destination that He wills for us!

_____
_____
_____
_____
_____

May 13

Filled Up

I changed the oil in my car the other day; after about twelve
hundred miles, it was a quart low. I didn't realize it until I
checked it. On the day of Pentecost, there were one hundred
twenty believers in the upper room. Acts 2:4 says, "They
were all filled with the Holy Spirit and began to speak with
other tongues, as the Spirit gave them utterance." Acts 4:31
says, "And when they had prayed, the place where they were
assembled together was shaken; and they were all filled with
the Holy Spirit..." They were filled in Acts chapter two, but
needed another filling in Acts chapter four. You May have
been filled in the past, but check your level now to see if
you're filled. Pray in tongues every day to stay filled up and
built up (1 Corinthians 14:4).

_____
_____
_____
_____
_____

May 14

Shine Bright

My little girl and I were riding down the road one night, and she said, "Daddy, some headlights are brighter than others, why is it that way?" I told her it was because of the new halogen headlights they've come out with in the last few years; they are thirty percent brighter than a regular headlight. In Proverbs 4:18, the Amplified Bible says, "The path of the [uncompromisingly] just and righteous is like the light of dawn, that shines more and more [brighter and clearer]." Don't compromise your faith; be brighter and clearer for Christ. Tell people about Him, and shine bright. Don't be a regular headlight - be like a halogen and shine bright!

_____

_____

_____

_____

_____

May 15

Who Will You Serve

In these latter days that we are in, the church of Jesus Christ is being hit right and left, day after day, on how we feel about certain issues facing our society. In 1 Kings 18:21, Elijah came to the people and said, "How long will you falter between two opinions? If the Lord is God, follow Him; but if Baal, follow him. But the people answered him not a word." It is so easy to lay back and not say a word, and then the devil takes over the situation. Speak up, Church! Tell them Jesus Christ loves them, and wants them to come to Him before it's too late.

_____

_____

_____

_____

_____

May 16

Life Insurance

I talked to a man one time who told me he needed some term life insurance for his family and himself. I told him that is a wonderful idea for financial security for this life, but asked him if he had ever thought about spiritual life insurance for the next life? In 2 Corinthians 4:18, the Bible says, "While we do not look at the things which are seen, but at the things which are not seen..." I told him he could have eternal life in Jesus Christ. All he would have to do is repent and ask Jesus to come into his heart. That would be like signing on the dotted line to make the life insurance policy valid, and then his name would be recorded in the Lamb's Book of Life!

_____

_____

_____

_____

_____

May 17

Busybodies

Have you ever run into some people in your walk with the Lord that are busybodies? They know everything about everybody in the church; they have a lot of time on their hands. They are the Christian soap opera of the church; they know every episode down to the smallest detail on what so-and-so did. Their program would be called "The Deceiving Light". In 2 Thessalonians 3:11, the Bible says, "For we hear that there are some who walk among you in a disorderly manner, not working at all, but are busybodies." I really believe the way we can keep this soap opera from jumping on us is to get involved in the church working for the Lord; then you'll find yourself delivered from "the deceiving light".

_____
_____
_____
_____
_____

May 18

Bathroom

I walked into this bathroom one time, and saw all this profanity written on the walls. I said, "Lord, that is terrible;" He said, "Yes it is, now put a gospel tract on the wall to give the people something good to read." In Isaiah 55:11 the Bible says "So shall My word be that goes forth from My mouth; It shall not return to Me void, but it shall accomplish what I please, and it shall prosper in the thing for which I sent it." A guy told me one time a man gave a tract to him; he started to throw it away like all the rest, but this stuck to his hand. He tried to shake it off, but it stayed there - he read the tract and got saved!

_____
_____
_____
_____
_____

May 19

Standing Up

Have you ever stopped to realize in these days we are in, that a lot of people are upset at us Christians, just because we love Jesus? Some Christians are falling away because of the persecution, but persecution is good for you- to develop you for more persecution. In 2 Corinthians 4:7-10, Paul said, "We have this treasure in earthen vessels... We are hard-pressed on every side, yet not crushed; perplexed, but not in despair; persecuted, but not forsaken; struck down, but not destroyed- always carrying about in the body the dying of the Lord Jesus, that the life of Jesus may be manifested in us." The degree of our commitment to Christ is based upon our confession of Him - in times of great persecution.

_____
_____
_____
_____
_____

May 20

Tested Word

Have you realized as a Christian that the life you live says who you really are? In Revelation 12:11 the Bible says, "And they overcame him by the blood of the Lamb and by the word of their testimony..." "Testimony" means word-tested. Has the Word been tested in you- has it been tested in your life? The world is not interested in how much we know; but they are impressed when we live what we know. That person that is giving you a hard time is testing you; you are being refined in the fire, for the next opportunity to be tested. You're not losing ground - you're gaining ground!

May 21

Abortion

I just can't understand how a born-again Christian, who says they love Jesus with all their heart, can be pro-choice on the subject of abortion. In Psalm 139:13 the Bible says, "For you formed my inward parts; you covered me in my mother's womb." In Jeremiah 1:5 it says, "Before I formed you in the womb I knew you..." I think we need to be bold in these evil times, and speak forth the Word of God. It's murder based on greed; it's a big business. Ask your Pastor how he believes in this area; if he wants to shrug the issue and not take a stand - you may need to find another Pastor with a backbone that will.

May 22

You Have Risen

Do you recall when you first got saved, your friends would come up to you and say things like, "We were at the dance hall the other night and didn't see you", or "Wednesday night is our regular poker night and you were not there. We came by Joe's Bar and Grill on Friday afternoon for our usual couple of beers and you weren't there." In Luke 24:-5-6 the Bible says, "...Why do you seek the living among the dead? He is not here, but is risen!" They were looking for you in the dead places; but you had risen, and now you are alive. You don't do what you used to do, or hang out in dead places, because you have risen. Everything is new, the old is passed away. There are new places to hang out and new places to go - tell them you have risen!

_____

_____

_____

_____

_____

May 23

Who You Know

Have you ever heard the old saying "It's not what you know, but it's who you know"? If you want to buy a car, and you know the owner of the dealership, he may give you a good deal. When a father comes home late at night, and knocks on the door and says, "Honey, let me in"; she recognizes his voice because she knows him. In John 10:4 Jesus said, "And when he brings out his own sheep, he goes before them; and the sheep follow him, for they know his voice." So many people today are trying to rub shoulders with the world, for special privileges. Let's stay with Jesus; because when we knock on His door, He always opens - because He knows our voice. I would rather know Him.

_____

_____

_____

_____

_____

May 24

Stone Rolled Away

Have you ever stopped to think, that all of us got saved by somebody praying for us? In John 11:38, Jesus was groaning in Himself and came to Lazarus" tomb; it was a cave and a stone lay against it. We were in a tomb before we were saved; the stone was the blindfold that was on our eyes, we couldn't see. Lazarus was in there four days, and he did not smell very good; we used to stink with the smell of sin. Jesus told Mary in verse forty, that if she would believe she would see the glory of God. Then He said, "Lazarus, come forth!" Someone believed God for us, and we came forth. We took the grave clothes of the old man off, and put on the new clothes of the new man. Jesus said, "Loose him and let him go." Go forth, Church and preach - because you have risen!

_____

_____

_____

_____

_____

May 25

Backslider

Can you think of someone right now, who has slipped away from the Lord, or who has never received Jesus? In Matthew 18:11-14, Jesus said He has come to save those that are lost. He says if you have a hundred sheep, and one goes straying off and you find it; that you rejoice more over that one, than the ninety-nine that did not go astray. If the Lord has laid someone on your heart, go to them, and bring them back home. They really want you to visit them; they are lonely and feel rejected. Let's go out, and get them in - and welcome them home.

_____

_____

_____

_____

_____

May 26

Laughing

I went to a meeting recently, and the brother that was speaking read Psalm 126:2, which says, "Then our mouth was filled with laughter, and our tongue with singing..." He said, "You think nothing of it when the song leader leads you in praise and worship, and you start singing. Why don't we laugh in the spirit?" Well they started laughing, and it wasn't long before close to two thousand people were laughing. If you feel depressed or sad at times, start laughing and singing. It will seem strange at first starting out; but you'll slip into the spirit, and off you go - the devil can't stand it!

_____

_____

_____

_____

_____

May 27

Oil

My next-door neighbor was trying to start her lawnmower, and it wouldn't start. Well, I jumped the fence to see if I could help. I noticed she had no oil in the lawnmower. I put some oil in it, and it started and ran beautifully. In Psalm 92:10 the Bible says, "...I have been anointed with fresh oil." If you have trouble getting started, check your oil; you may need to add some fresh oil. You'll be running so smooth, that people may ask what kind of oil you use - it's the oil of gladness.

_____
_____
_____
_____
_____

May 28

Labor Pains

We have two beautiful children, and I was talking to my wife one time about the delivering of the children. What was it like giving birth? She said that right before the baby is delivered, you feel like quitting because you're so exhausted. We as Christians should be pregnant with souls. In Psalm 126:5 the Bible says, "Those who sow in tears shall reap in joy." My wife said, "Honey, when I saw the baby delivered, the pain was worth it; I was happy." Don't stop praying for those God is laying on your heart. Yes, you feel as if you want to quit, but they are on the way. When you see them delivered from Satan's trap, because you've prayed - the joy will be there!

May 29

In the Mall

My daughter Melanie and I were walking through the mall one day.

Four boys came walking by, and one of them wanting to flirt with Melanie, said "Hi, I'm Elvis Presley." The Holy Spirit just rose up in me; I turned to the four of them and said, "Hi, I'm a Christian - do you know Jesus?" They had egg all over their face; one of them was not saved, and he invited Jesus into his heart. The devil is so stupid; he opened his mouth - and we took advantage of the situation. In 2 Timothy 4:2 the Bible says, "Preach the word! Be ready in season and out of season..."

_____
_____
_____
_____
_____

May 30

Going Home

It is so easy sometimes to get discouraged; people are criticizing you because you're a Christian, they can't understand your motives. Every day, it seems like a new level of persecution hits you. But we have to realize that we are not of this world. In John 14:2 Jesus said, "In My Father's house are many mansions... I go to prepare a place for you." It's so exciting to read God's Word, and see the promises that await us in heaven. Through His love and promises, we can have heaven here on earth; enjoy what the Lord has for you now. This will help when the trials come, which are opportunities to show forth God's power. Hang in there, Church - because it won't be long until we are going home!

_____

_____

_____

_____

_____

May 31

Bitterness

There is so much going on in these latter days that we are in; it is so important that we stay in prayer and in love, with one another. In the natural, it's hard to pray for someone that's giving you a hard time; if we are in the spirit, it's so much easier. In Hebrews 12:12 the Bible says, "Strengthen the hands which hang down, and the feeble knees." Verse fifteen says, "...lest any root of bitterness springing up cause trouble, and by this become defiled." Just forgive, and His love will flow. The Lord is doing some mighty things today, and He wants to use us. Be careful that you don't become bitter - and you will become better.

_____
_____
_____
_____
_____

June 1

Attitude

My wife asked me to do something the other day, and I said, "Yes Sugar, I'll get it." She said, "You've been saying that for I don't know how long. When are you going to do it?" Well it was just a little thing, but I just had a bad attitude about doing it. In 1 Peter 3:7-8 the Bible says, "Husbands, likewise, dwell with them with understanding, giving honor to the wife, as to the weaker vessel, and as being heirs together of the grace of life, that your prayers May not be hindered." It is so good how the Word of God straightens us out; it will always hit us right where we need it - your attitude determines your altitude!

_____
_____
_____
_____
_____

June 2

Concrete

We were sharing Jesus on the streets the other night, and we came up to four young college girls, and started talking to them about the love of Jesus. If you could have heard the things that came out of their mouth, it would amaze you. One of them claimed to be Jesus, and another one thought it was okay to live together and not be married. They were cursing and just really bold about their sin; they said there is no hell, and denied the Bible was true. 2 Timothy 4:4 says, "They will turn their ears away from the truth..." It was like their minds were like concrete, thoroughly mixed and well set; but we realized the Word of God was powerful, and would pierce through and hit the heart. Have you ever noticed concrete - sometimes grass will grow right through it?

_____

_____

_____

_____

_____

June 3

Sweet Smelling

Did you realize that when you praise the Lord God, He is eating and drinking from that offering you are lifting up to Him? In Revelation 3:20 Jesus said, "Behold, I stand at the door and knock. If anyone hears My voice and opens the door, I will come in to him and dine with him, and he with Me." When you worship and tell Him you love Him, you are dining together. We are always wanting to be fed; the Lord wants to be fed, too. Your praises, prayers, lifestyle, and words that you say, are feeding a sweet aroma to Him; and in turn, He feeds you with His love. That means more than anything. Sit down at the table with Him; offer Him the meat, potatoes, and vegetables - and then get some for you!

June 4

Fishing for God

I know you are familiar with the verse in Matthew 4:19 where Jesus said, "I'll make you fishers of men." Have you ever tried to clean a fish before you caught it? When a new convert comes to Jesus, everybody wants to clean him up. It takes time to do it right; the Holy Spirit is a wonderful fish cleaner. It may lay there awhile and stink, but He knows how to make it smell better. He also knows when to remove the scales, how much seasoning needs to be applied, how hot the oven needs to be, and then on the table, ready to eat. Are you ready now - for the world to taste you?

_____

_____

_____

_____

_____

June 5

Air Conditioner

My air conditioner went out, and it was in the high nineties. It was a whole week without the cool stuff, that we had taken so much for granted. After a few days of God dealing with our attitudes, we we're starting to adjust to the situation, and go on with life. In Philippians 4:11, Paul says, (NIV) "I am not saying this because I am in need, for I have learned to be content whatever the circumstances." When we started putting our eyes on Him, instead of on the heat - it got a lot cooler!

_____

_____

_____

_____

_____

June 6

Steady Spirit

Did you know that you can have a shaky flesh and a steady spirit at the same time? That's where so many of us fall short, because we back up and don't push through. It doesn't make any difference how you feel, you have to say "Flesh, we are going whether you like it or not." The Lord told me one time to walk in the middle of a crowd of people and preach; my flesh was afraid, but my spirit was willing. In Romans 8:15 the Bible says, (NIV) "You did not receive a spirit that makes you a slave again to fear..." Fear didn't leave, until I made the move to go with my spirit. The flesh will always be shaky - but your spirit is steady.

June 7

Butterfly

My daughter is in this singing group at school. She says she gets butterflies sometimes right before she sings; I have them myself sometimes before I preach. In 1 Corinthians 2:10 the Bible says, "...the Spirit searches all things, yes, the deep things of God." 2 Corinthians 2:14 says, (NIV) "Thanks be to God who always leads us in triumphal procession in Christ, and through us spreads everywhere the fragrance of the knowledge of Him." Yes, those butterflies may be there; but God is leading us through a triumphal procession, because the Spirit searches all things. Just let Him have His way. When I see her using her talents in playing the piano or singing, my heart is full of joy. Remember, butterflies are okay - but you have to get them in the right formation!

_____

_____

_____

_____

_____

June 8

Holy Ghost Copies

Have you ever thought about how a copier works? You put your material in to be copied, push the button; a bright light shines to produce an image, out comes a copy of the original. In Genesis 1:26 God said, "Let Us make man in Our own image..." He wanted to put a copy of Himself on the earth. But man fell into sin, and his image was like that of Satan; this was an evil copy going throughout all mankind. Jesus" death on the cross and rising from the dead produced an image of light to us; now we are that copy through the shed Blood. Go to church, and put your image out there - make as many copies as you like.

_____

_____

_____

_____

_____

June 9

Aroma

I came into the kitchen the other night, and my wife had some chili brewing on the stove. Oh, the aroma from that chili smelled so good. In 2 Corinthians 2:15-16 the Bible says, (NIV) "For we are to God the aroma of Christ among those who are being saved and those who are perishing." The aroma drew me to the table, where the chili put life in my flesh. If you keep rejecting the aroma of food and do not eat, you will die. We are the aroma for the world; they need to smell the sweet fragrance of the gospel, sit down at the table of salvation, and eat freely. The way you live your life will determine the right aroma. That chili had some hot stuff in it, too; it tastes better when it's hot (spicy) - the aroma goes further!

_____
_____
_____
_____
_____

June 10

Being Real

Have you ever noticed on Sunday mornings when you go to church, how nice everyone is? Everyone seems so loving and spiritual; you are having a wonderful time. Then suddenly on the way home, the kids get to fighting in the back seat...you want to go home, your wife wants to go out to eat...it's ninety degrees outside, and the air conditioner is broken on the car. James 1:2-3 says, (NIV) "Consider it pure joy, my brothers, whenever you face trials of many kinds, because you know the testing of your faith develops perseverance." Isn't it wonderful, how God helps us in these times of testing - aren't you excited that another one is just around the corner?

_____
_____
_____
_____
_____

June 11

Setting Straight

Have you ever had a little disagreement with someone, and both of you left angry? You would wake up in the morning, and this person would be on your mind. It's like a nagging fly buzzing around your head; the longer that fly nags you, the worse it gets. In Mark 11:25 the Bible says, (NIV) "And when you stand praying, if you hold anything against anyone, forgive him, so that your Father in heaven May forgive you your sins." If you want that fly to leave, forgive them; and you ask them to forgive you. If you don't, that fly will bring more flies, to jump on everyone you come in contact with. Let's have a clean environment - by forgiving.

_____

_____

_____

_____

June 12

Clothes

When you get ready to go to work in the morning, I am sure you want to look your best; your clothes need to look nice, in order for you to make a good outward impression. What about your spiritual clothes that you put on? In Isaiah 61:3, the Bible says to put on the garment of praise for the spirit of heaviness. Verse ten says, (NIV) "...He has clothed me with the garments of salvation, and arrayed me in a robe of righteousness..." When these clothes are put on every day, your outward appearance will look much better. Put off the old way of living - and put on the new man!

_____
_____
_____
_____
_____

June 13

Fishing

I was at work one day, and the guys were talking about how many fish they caught Sunday. I spoke up and said, "I caught twenty-two fish that weighed from one hundred thirty to two hundred pounds, at the Richmond City Jail last night." In Matthew 4:19-20, Jesus said, "Follow Me, and I will make you fishers of men." They immediately left their nets and followed him. Did you notice that Peter was a fisherman? But Jesus said, "I'll make you fishers of men." The world doesn't mind you talking about catching bass, catfish, or spot; but when you mention catching men for Jesus, they get upset. They are just afraid if they hang around the bait, they're going to get hooked one day; and they are exactly right. The bait that we put on our hooks - is the best you can get.

June 14

Good Intentions

I was talking to a man about Jesus one day, and he said, "Hank, I know I am a sinner, and I know I need to get saved. My life is not peaceful, but Jesus knows my heart. I'll get around to it one of these days." In Joel 3:14 the Bible says, "Multitudes, multitudes in the valley of decision!" There are so many people in the valley of decision; they mean well, but they just haven't said yes to Jesus. We are in the latter days; Jesus could come at any time. My heart was sad when he said, "I know what I need to do, but I'll wait." Church, don't stop telling the good news - keep it up! The world has stepped up its attack on the church; we need to step up our attack. The road to hell is paved with good intentions.

_____

_____

_____

_____

_____

June 15

Dancing

Did you realize the devil can't stand for you to be happy? You take the subject of dancing; now before you were saved, he didn't mind if you danced and looked like a fool, because everybody else was doing it. But the moment you got saved, and went to a church that danced in the spirit, he'll do everything he can to keep you from doing it. In Psalm 150:4, the Bible says to praise Him with the timbrel and dance. Well if you sing and play instruments in church, why not dance? Before you were saved you didn't think anything of it; why let it bother you now? Some churches are like funeral homes. If you act happy in there, they think your elevator doesn't go to the top floor; but they are the ones bound up and don't realize it. I don't care what people think - I care what He thinks.

June 16

Consuming God

I was looking at TV one day about the power of volcanoes. It showed the lava flowing down the side of the mountain, consuming everything in its path- trees, houses, bridges, nothing was left. Deuteronomy 4:24 says our God is a consuming fire. He consumed the devil at Calvary. He consumed sin, sickness, anger, strife, confusion, lust; all the things the devil represented, He consumed them. You may be thinking, how I am going to overcome the situation I'm in? Let Jesus have it, and watch Him consume it. Nothing stood in the way of hot lava consuming everything in its path; and no devil from hell can stop the power of God, from consuming everything that's not of Him. He is awesome - give Him a chance!

_____
_____
_____
_____
_____

June 17

Standing Up

Have you noticed lately how upset people are getting, when you say what the Bible says about certain subjects? It's fun to stand up for Jesus, but the devil gets upset. Some people don't want to be around you; it's like you have the plague or something. In Matthew 5:11-12 Jesus said, "Blessed are you when they revile and persecute you and say all kinds of evil against you falsely for My sake. Rejoice and be exceedingly glad, for great is your reward..." Stand up Church, and be happy. It may look like they have the upper hand, but time is running out for the devil - and he knows it. The Church is the only thing that's going to be left standing, when the battle is over.

_____

_____

_____

_____

_____

June 18

Stand Guard

I was in a department store the other day, and I noticed a policemen standing guard. He was making sure nobody was going to steal some merchandise from the store. Did you know that the devil tries to steal from you? But you can stand guard; in Song of Solomon 2:15 the Bible says "Catch the foxes for us, the little foxes ruining the vines, while our vineyards are in blossom." You can get rid of these foxes by using the name of Jesus. Humble yourself before God, and watch the Holy Spirit run them out of your vineyard. So stand guard - and produce lots of fruit for Christ.

June 19

Dig Out the Areas

I was watching it snow the other day, and it was so beautiful, as it built up inch by inch. A few hours later, I couldn't see the road or my driveway; they were hidden. It wasn't until I took the snow shovel and dug, that I could find the driveway. We have to be willing to dig out areas of our lives that are hidden. In Matthew 5:8 the Bible says, "Blessed are the pure in heart, for they shall see God." I didn't see my driveway until I started digging; let Jesus dig out the areas that He is not pleased with, so you can see Him and be blessed. Don't let these things pile up - inch by inch.

June 20

Clean and Wrinkle-Free

I went to the cleaners the other day to pick up my suit. As I was taking it to the car, I noticed all the wrinkles were gone, and it looked so nice and clean. That's the way Jesus wants us to look spiritually, clean and wrinkle-free. In 2 Corinthians 10:4 the Bible says, "For the weapons of our warfare are not carnal but mighty in God for pulling down strongholds." When we try to fight the devil on our own strength, we get all wrinkled up. It says we can be mighty through God, to pull down any strongholds. So if you look all wrinkled up, take yourself to the cleaners - and let Jesus press them out!

_____
_____
_____
_____
_____

June 21

Gifts Under the Tree

I had a wonderful Christmas this year, getting together with family members exchanging gifts; but the greatest gift of all, was God's gift to us. In Ephesians 2:8 the Bible says, "For by grace you have been saved through faith, and that not of yourselves; it is the gift of God." If we aren't careful during the Christmas season, we can get so caught up with the world. They are rushing, fighting one another for parking spaces, and getting into debt by buying too many gifts. If we aren't careful, we forget the real meaning of Christmas. We put our gifts under the tree; God put His gift for us on the tree - let's remember that every day of the year.

_____

_____

_____

_____

_____

June 22

Keep Looking

Did you know that the world is looking at you? If they know that you are a Christian, they are looking at you, to see if you are able to stand the pressure. In James 1:2-3 the Bible says, "My brethren, count it all joy when you fall into divers temptations; knowing this, that the trying of your faith worketh patience." Let the world look at you, so they can see the presence of God in that situation. Don't get upset when they give you a hard time; count it all joy. Most of them want what you have anyway, so let them look at you; if they keep looking long enough – they'll get saved!

June 23

Last Minute

We have such a wonderful God, He takes care of us.
In Matthew 7:8 the Bible says, "For everyone who asks
receives, and he who seeks finds, and to him who knocks
it will be opened." Have you ever prayed for something or
someone, and thanked the Lord for answering your prayer-
because by faith it's done? Weeks and months go by, and
it hasn't come to pass yet. Hold on, and keep holding on,
because it's coming; He said, "Ask and you will receive."
Your faith brings it to pass; don't beg God, just thank Him
and forget it. He sometimes comes through on the last minute
- but He is never late.

_____

_____

_____

_____

_____

June 24

Flesh

Have you ever noticed yourself at times slipping in the flesh; and it seems as if the old devil has taken another bite, and slowly eating away at you? In Romans 8:6, the Bible says the mind set on the flesh is death, but the mind set on the Spirit is life and peace. Whatever you set your mind on, before long you will be living what you are thinking. When you got saved, it is no longer your nature to live in the flesh. Romans 8:13 says, "For if you live according to the flesh you will die; but if by the Spirit you put to death the deeds of the body, you will live." If you give God all of you - the devil has nothing to eat!

_____
_____
_____
_____
_____

June 25

Able

Have you ever been before the Lord, and He's impressed upon your heart to do something for Him; and you've replied, "Lord, I don't have the ability to do that"? Did you know He is not interested in your ability, but availability? 2 Corinthians 3:4-6 says such confidence we have through Christ, who also qualified us "...as ministers of the new covenant, not of the letter but of the Spirit..." If He's called you to do something, He'll qualify you to do it. So make yourself available for the job - and let His ability flow through you.

_____
_____
_____
_____
_____

June 26

Spectator-itis

Mark 16:15 says, "Go into all the world and preach the gospel." That means wherever you are, share Jesus. Well if you are a Christian, chances are you've shared on the job. That means the world is looking at you, and wants to know where you stand on every controversial issue facing us today. They will ask you, where do you stand on homosexuality, abortion, and capital punishment? Are you going to be bold and say what God says about it, or get spectator-itis? "Spectator-itis" is a disease that comes on Christians when we back up and don't stand up. Speak always what the Bible says - and spectator-itis will not be a problem!

June 27

Supply and Demand

Did you notice that during the Gulf War, there were over five hundred thousand troops there? When they went to war with Iraq, those troops on the front lines had to have supplies; so they ask for them, or their mission would not be effective. When you go to the bank, you are drawing from your supply; when Jesus died for us on the cross, He deposited salvation in the bank. Philippians 4:19 says, "God shall supply all your need according to His riches in glory through Christ Jesus." Go to the bank, lay your faith card down there, and say "Jesus, I'd like to make a withdrawal from my account." He has the supply - we need to make the request.

_____

_____

_____

_____

_____

June 28

Enter and Leave

Did you know that all you ever do in life, is enter and leave? You enter when you were born, and you will leave when you die; you enter into your house at night, and leave for work in the morning. Everywhere we go, we enter and leave. In Revelation 3:20, Jesus says He stands at the door and knocks, if anyone opens the door He will come in. When Jesus finished His work, He left with a blaze of glory. One day we will have to leave; let's be faithful to Him each day, because the day for leaving is drawing near. Everyone is in a hurry today, no one wants to leave. This world has nothing to offer but frustration; we have the message of hope. Let's point the way for them to enter - and the way they leave will be so much better!

_____
_____
_____
_____
_____

June 29

Not Lost

Have you ever heard about this traveling salesman that drove into a small town, and saw this little boy standing on the corner? He said "Son, do you know where a good restaurant is?" The boy replied, "No, sir." "Do you know where the local garage is?" The little boy replied, "No sir." "Do you know where a motel is?" The boy replied, "No sir." Finally out of frustration, the salesman replied, "Do you know anything, Boy?" The boy replied, "I'm not lost." In 1 Corinthians 13:12 the Bible says, "Now I know in part, but then I shall know..." You're going to have a lot of questions thrown at you in these latter days, and you may not have all the answers; but one thing you can tell them – you're not lost.

_____
_____
_____
_____
_____

June 30

Alarm Clock

Just about everyone has an alarm clock; you set it for the time you want to wake up. Just when you're sleeping good, that thing goes off, time to wake up and go to work. The church in America has been asleep on the abortion issue; God has been raising up alarm clocks all over America, to stand in front of abortion clinics and sound the alarm. In Ephesians 5:14 God says, "Awake you who sleep, arise from the dead, and Christ will give you light." When the church sees this on TV, newspapers, and radio, it's an alarm clock going off from God saying, "Wake up, time to wake up;" and He will give you light when you stand up. The anointing will fall, and you will be an alarm clock going off in somebody's ear. We don't like alarm clocks sometimes - but they sure are needed!

_____
_____
_____
_____
_____

July 1

Foot Caught

Have you ever realized that fear can grip you so hard, that you do not know what's happening? Fear is not trusting in God to take care of your problem. In Proverbs 3:5 the Bible says, "Trust in the Lord with all your heart, and lean not on your own understanding." It's when we lean on our understanding that we get in trouble. The devil isn't our problem; it's our thought life. If we change our thinking on His Word instead of the problem, our confidence builds; and our foot will not get caught in Satan's trap. He will get you if you fear - but perfect love casts out fear.

_____

_____

_____

_____

_____

July 2

Ransom

If someone came to your house, took your son or daughter, and wanted you to pay money to get them back...you love them so much, that you would give all you had financially to get them back. The devil deceived Adam and Eve, and they were captured by him. God paid the ransom by sending His son Jesus to shed that precious blood, to buy us back into fellowship with Him. Can you imagine that son or daughter, how happy they would be when rescued? I can still remember how happy I was, when Jesus rescued me. Luke 2:11 says, "For there is born to you this day in the city of David a Savior, who is Christ the Lord." Thank you, Jesus - for paying the price for us!

_____
_____
_____
_____
_____

July 3

Twenty Percent Bible

I was talking to a man the other day about Jesus; he said eighty percent of the Bible is a lie and was written by man, only about twenty percent of it is true. I asked him could he believe twenty percent of the Bible, and he said yes. I said, do you believe Jesus was virgin-born and died on the cross for your sins; he said, yes I do. Well what's stopping you from praying right now to receive Jesus, on twenty percent of what you believe? Well, he didn't know what to say; he didn't get saved, but it got him thinking. In Revelation 2:7 the Lord said, "He who has an ear, let him hear what the Spirit says to the churches..." We must be willing to feed them where they are. When they receive Him - they will be one hundred percent believers.

July 4

Pride

We are receiving some good teaching in many different areas in this country; we are so blessed, that we can be spoiled if not careful. We have to constantly give it out to someone. If not, we will think that we have arrived to such a spiritual plateau, that we are of no value for anyone. Galatians 6:3 says "For if anyone thinks himself to be something, when he is nothing, he deceives himself." A person who thinks he's arrived wants to straighten everyone else out; but he doesn't want to look in the mirror at himself. As long as you realize that you haven't arrived, He will take you where you need to go. If you think you have arrived - you will never get where He wants you to go!

_____
_____
_____
_____
_____

July 5

Life Speaks

What will your life say after you are gone? The things that you are doing now, will they speak of your love for Jesus years after you're gone? Hebrews 11:4 says "By faith Abel offered to God a more excellent sacrifice than Cain, through which he obtained witness that he was righteous, God testifying of his gifts; and through it he being dead still speaks." In James 2:20 the Bible says faith without works is dead. Your true faith in Christ will be followed by works that will glorify the Lord, not you. And when you graduate and go home to be with Him - as with Abel, your life will speak long after you are gone.

_____

_____

_____

_____

_____

July 6

Being Delicate

Medical doctors just amaze me sometimes; I was looking at a program on TV the other day, and they were performing an operation on a young man's brain. The slightest move the wrong way by the doctor could have caused so much damage; he had to be delicate with his instruments. That's how we have to be in ministering to people; we want to do surgery on these heads, and we are operating in the wrong area. Just listening sometimes and not saying a word, they will tell us where the problem is. Then we can pull out our medicine bag, the Word of God. Then reach in and apply the right instrument or scripture, that will go to their heart with love - before their head knows what is happening. That's delicate surgery!

July 7

Lies

It is so wonderful to be saved, in love with Jesus; and at the same time in a world that hates you, because you love Him. It gets discouraging sometimes, and we make mistakes in this journey we are on; but He is always there to help us out of the mess. Hosea 14:4 says He will heal their backsliding. Don't you lay down there and dwell on your mistakes; come back to Jesus, and let Him heal you. Spend time talking the Bible, instead of thinking on your mistakes. Healing will come, confidence will be there, and boldness will show forth. The light will be back on, and the devil will say, "Let me get out of here - they are dangerous."

July 8

Contentment

Are you content with your life now? Do you feel that real peace on the inside? In 1 Timothy 6:6 the Bible says, "Now godliness with contentment is great gain." The devil does everything he can to get you out of that state of contentment. Now the word "contention" means strife, of a position taken in an argument. Everything around us today is in contention; but we are the ones that can share the message of contentment, to bring them great gain. Yes, we feel the pressure every day. Give it to Jesus, and have fun being saved and free from contention - but being content!

_____

_____

_____

_____

_____

July 9

War

I noticed something on TV the other day, when the missiles started to come in to invade; the sirens started to go off to warn everyone to take cover. In 1 Thessalonians 5:22 the Bible says, "Abstain from every form of evil." When the devil tempts you with wrong, a warning siren goes off on the inside saying, "Watch out- this isn't good." That's the Holy Spirit warning you; get away fast, before the missile attacks. If you hang around in enemy territory, they will take you POW; you will be a prisoner of war. Psalm 50:15 says, "Call upon Me in the day of trouble; I will deliver thee..." He will send the commandoes (the angels) to set you free. Let's keep the good fight of faith, and at the same time be sensitive to the sirens - to warn us of incoming missiles.

_____
_____
_____
_____
_____

July 10

Gloomy and Sad

Have you noticed how gloomy and sad, so many people are today? Even as Christians, if we aren't careful, we can look at the situation around us; and that thick cloud of gloom and despair comes over us. On the other hand, we can look at God's Word, and see the situation in a different way. In Psalm 56:3 the Bible says, "Whenever I am afraid I will trust in You." The skies are clear, and you can see which way He wants you to go. So look up and praise Him; thank Him and trust Him. It's so good to love Him - no matter what the weather is like!

July 11

Pure in Heart

It is so exciting to be alive today; without Jesus, we couldn't stand all the pressure put on the church. The world is looking at us, and we need to watch ourselves. Men, have you noticed the closer we get to God, the devil sends his agents out to try to destroy us? In Proverbs 5:3 the Bible says, "For the lips of an immoral woman drip honey, and her mouth is smoother than oil." Watch out for those slick-talking women- that want to praise the Lord out of one side of their mouth, and try to flirt with you with the other side. In Proverbs 5:8 it says, "Remove your way far from her." Don't counsel alone with her; have your wife with you, or a third person. Proverbs 5:5 says, "Her feet go down to death, her steps lay hold of hell." Remember guys; keep pure before Him - because He sees everything we do.

July 12

Give Gospel

Whenever I look at the Bible on giving, I see that it says if I give, He will take care of me. In Matthew 6:19-20, Jesus was telling us to lay up treasures in heaven and not on the earth. Material things can become like gods to us, if we aren't careful. Verse 21 says "Where your treasure is, there your heart will be also." In Philippians 4:19, the Bible says He will meet all our needs according to His riches in glory through Christ Jesus. Put Jesus first in everything you do, and He will take care of you. Give to Him because you love Him, and "...all these things will be added unto you" (Matt. 6:33). Whatever you need to fulfill His will, will be there on time - H.P.S. - Heavenly Parcel Post!

_____
_____
_____
_____
_____

July 13

Naked Before Him

Before Adam and Eve sinned, they were naked before God and in perfect fellowship with Him. After they sinned, they realized their nakedness and were ashamed before Him. In Genesis 3:7 the Bible says, "The eyes of both of them were opened, and they knew that they were naked; and they sewed fig leaves together and made themselves coverings." Are you covering something up in your life, that you don't want God to see? Don't hide from Him; give your sin to Him- He already knows you're doing it. If the Word of God through His Spirit says you're wrong, repent; don't cover it up. Be naked before Him - and He will lift you up, and clothe you with righteousness.

_____
_____
_____
_____
_____

July 14

No-Name Army

God is raising up a no-name army in these latter days. This no-name army will be anointed to preach the gospel, heal the sick, cast out demons, and raise the dead. This no-name army will be lifting up one name, that precious name of Jesus. Acts 4:12 says, "Nor is there salvation in any other, for there is no other name under heaven given among men by which we must be saved." They can't get saved in your name, but only in His name. God is raising a no-name army; the world is going to be saying, where did these people come from? I've never heard their names before. You will not be known - but He will be known in this no-name army!

_____

_____

_____

_____

_____

July 15

Die to Live

Did you know that we live to die, and we die to live? Romans 6:7 says, "For he who has died has been freed from sin." If we have been freed from sin, then how does sin creep up in our lives from time to time? In Romans 6:11-12, "Likewise you also, consider yourselves to be dead indeed to sin, but alive to God in Christ Jesus our Lord. Therefore do not let sin reign in your mortal body, that you should obey it in its lusts." You have to consider yourself dead. So to live in Christ is to die to self, and to die is to live in Him. Let's keep on dying, and we'll keep on living; if we keep on living - then we'll keep on dying.

_____

_____

_____

_____

_____

July 16

You Have What You Say

How can you expect to be healthy, if you are eating bad food? Junk food will produce junk, if that's your main diet; a bad confession will produce a bad attitude. In Proverbs 18:21 the Bible says, "Death and life are in the power of the tongue, and those who love it will eat its fruit." If you are always negative and critical, just being an old sour puss, then you are death walking around in a body. If on the other hand you start speaking positive things, uplifting one another, life will be coming out of you. Your wife and children will be saying, "Daddy sure looks healthy today - he must be eating the right food!"

_____
_____
_____
_____
_____

July 17

Boiling Water

A good friend of mine has a seafood business; he gave me a bunch of clams one time. I said, "Warren, how do you open these things up?" He said, "Put them in boiling water, and after a few minutes they will open right up; put on a little salt and pepper, a little hot sauce, and have yourself a ball." We're just like those clams; we don't want to open up, until the pressure is on. Persecution is good for us. In Matthew 5:10 Jesus said, "Blessed are those who are persecuted for righteousness" sake, for theirs is the Kingdom of Heaven." When the devil puts you in a boiling situation, he thinks he's got you now; but that just causes us to open up, and share the love of Jesus even more. As long as you're standing up for Jesus, you will always be in hot water - but He says, "I will never leave you nor forsake you."

_____

_____

_____

_____

_____

July 18

Pride

Have you ever realized that pride is the result of believing lies about yourself? Humility is the result of believing truth about yourself. In Proverbs 16:18 the Bible says, "Pride goes before destruction, and a haughty spirit before a fall." Pride is so blinding; it will make you think that you have it all together; but in reality you're all messed up. Do not be wise in your own opinion. Pick your friends that are humble, stay away from the proud. Let's walk in reality, and be real. Pride loves from the head - humility loves from the heart.

_____
_____
_____
_____
_____

July 19

Bull and Lion

A brother told me one time that he had a dream; there was this bull and a lion. The bull was in the fence, and the lion was on the outside. Well as long as the bull was looking at the lion, he never would attack. This little chicken came through the fence, and started pecking at the bull's leg. After awhile, the blood was coming out of the bull's leg; the bull got weak, and the lion jumped the fence and attacked the bull. The brother woke up and said, "Lord, what does that mean?" The Lord said, "Go back to sleep." He had the same dream again; the bull was looking at the lion- here comes the chicken, pecking at the bull's leg. The bull raised his leg and squashed the chicken, and still kept looking at the lion! In James 1:2 the Bible says, "Count it all joy when you fall into various trails" - don't let the devil peck away at you!

July 20

Good Sinner

You know before I was saved, I was a real good sinner; I worked at it for a long time. I was good at cussing, good at drinking, partying, and having what I thought was a good time. Now that I am saved, that's all behind me. In James 1:22 the Bible says, "Be doers of the word, and not hearers only, deceiving yourselves." We need to be good at righteousness and godly living. We need to exercise the same enthusiasm for Jesus as we did before we were saved. I was working hard for the devil, and he about killed me. Now I am working hard for Jesus; but there is life, joy, peace, and happiness.
Let's be good Christians - not good sinners.

July 21

Mark of the Beast

I believe the biggest problem in the body of Christ today, is the majority of the saints are lukewarm. In Revelation 3:16 the Bible says, "Because you are lukewarm and neither cold nor hot, I will vomit you out of My mouth." So many people think that once you are saved, that's it. No, the decision is up to you whether you're going to continue on. I believe if you're lukewarm when the rapture takes place, you'll be left behind. In Revelation 2:4 it says, "Nevertheless I have this against you, that you have left your first love." Do you have that same zeal and fire that you had, when you first got saved? Ask Jesus to forgive you, and let the joy of the Lord restore your soul. Jeremiah 20:9 says, "...But His Word was in my heart like a burning fire..." Let His Word burn in your heart like fire; keep that child-like faith. The devil can't stand it - when you're hot for Jesus!

_____

_____

_____

_____

_____

July 22

Antichrist

Everybody today is trying to figure out who the Antichrist is. I don't care who he is, because when he comes on the scene, I believe I'll be gone. In 1 Thessalonians 4:17-18 it says, "We who are alive and remain shall be caught up together with them in the clouds to meet the Lord in the air... Therefore comfort one another with these words." That's what we're supposed to do, is "comfort one another with these words." Stop trying to figure who the antichrist is, and start comforting the saints. Yes, his coming is going to cause everyone who is left behind to receive his mark; but I've got news for him - Jesus is coming back and going to put a mark on him that he will never forget.

_____
_____
_____
_____
_____

July 23

Business

Did you know that a business with no sign out, is a sign of no business? Your main calling as a Christian is to advertise your sign; we want people to see whom we represent. I notice businesses, and they are always looking for ways to get the word out. We should be the same way; in Matthew 5:16 Jesus said, "Let your light shine before men..." If you have life in you, then your light has to shine; so your business as a Christian is to let your light shine. So put your sign out, and let them know you are in business - to give them some fire insurance!

July 24

Child as a Field

Have you ever noticed a farmer sowing seed? He takes a lot of time plowing the ground and getting it ready before planting. Our children are like that field. We spend a lot of time loving them, plowing at different times; giving them discipline, sowing seeds for that beautiful day, when the crop of fruit comes forth. In Matthew 13:38 Jesus said, "The field is the world..." We as parents have to be very careful of the wicked ones, trying to sow bad seeds into our children. At the same time, our lives have to be an example; so those seeds can take good root, and bear fruit. When you blow it, repent to your child; the seed is being watered. Your children will be tomorrow - what you put into them today.

_____
_____
_____
_____
_____

July 25

Miss a Meal

I was talking to a man the other day, and he said when he was growing up even though they were poor, they had three meals a day: oatmeal, cornmeal, and miss-a-meal. I thought I would roll over laughing. If we're not careful, we can talk like that at times, like we don't have anything. In Psalms 68:19 the Bible says, "Blessed be the Lord, who daily loads us with benefits..." He has blessed us so much, with salvation and the abundant life. Thank Him every day for blessing you with what you do have, and more will be added to bless others. I like oatmeal and cornmeal, but in Jesus I do not have to "miss a meal" - He fills me up!

_____

_____

_____

_____

_____

July 26

Oil Filter

Are you aware of what an oil filter does? It catches those fine impurities that can damage your engine. In Matthew 24:24 Jesus said, "For false christs and false prophets will rise and show great signs and wonders to deceive, if possible, even the elect." You have to read the Bible daily, as that is your filter. When a false teaching comes forth, you will be able to catch it- so it does not get into your spirit and damage your engine. False teaching first thrills, and then it kills; fascinates, then it assassinates. The more you know what the Bible says, the quicker you will notice what the devil says. The Bible will keep you away from sin, but sin will keep you away from the Bible. Keep your spirit clean - with the Holy Ghost filtering machine.

_____
_____
_____
_____
_____

July 27

Eating to Live

Have you ever realized how many Christian activities you have gone to, because a buffet was offered? Would you have gone if it wasn't a buffet? All you can eat; after the meal you're stuffed, you can't put your mind on the message. I am sure if we are really honest, all of us have been guilty of this. In Proverbs 23:20-21 the Bible says, "Do not mix with winebibbers, or with gluttonous eaters of meat; for the drunkard and the glutton will come to poverty, and drowsiness will clothe a man with rags." I don't think we have a problem with alcohol in the body of Christ, but gluttony is a problem. You may ask the question, how do I know when I am guilty of gluttony? Well, are you living to eat - or are you eating to live?

_____

_____

_____

_____

_____

July 28

Pressure

All of us as believers are going through so much pressure in these evil days. The world is getting darker, but the saints are getting brighter. Yes, because of pressure, it's so easy to sit back and let someone else do it. That's what the devil wants you to do. In 1 Peter 4:12-14 the Bible says, "Beloved, do not think it strange concerning the fiery trial which is to try you, as though some strange thing happened to you; but rejoice to the extent that you partake of Christ's sufferings, that when His glory is revealed, you may also be glad with exceeding joy." If you are insulted for the name of Christ, blessed are you, for the spirit of glory and of God rests upon you. On their part He is blasphemed, but on your part He is glorified. The greater the test - the greater your testimony!

July 29

His Name

I was witnessing to a man the other day about Jesus; I asked him if he knew Jesus as his Savior. He said "I'm a Baptist", and he started to talk about his church. When I asked him if he dies, does he know if he would go to heaven, he didn't know for sure. He was very proud of the Baptist name, but had trouble with the name of Jesus. It's okay to be Baptist, Pentecostal, or whatever, but make sure you know Jesus. When people ask me, I tell them I'm a Christian, that I love Jesus. In Acts 4:12 the Bible says, "...For there is no other name under heaven given among men by which we must be saved."
Be excited - pray for open doors to tell people about that name.

July 30

Children's Duties

I know a lot of young people today saying, "Hey, I just want to do my own thing." Well, as a Christian we can't do our own thing; we have to do His thing. Proverbs 10:1 says, "A wise son maketh a glad father, but a foolish son is the heaviness of his mother." I can remember as a young person when I did my own thing, how I got in so much trouble. I was a burden to them at times, and they had to smoke my britches to straighten me out; but I thank God today for it. Children, hang around kids that want to do the Lord's thing -because that is the only thing!

July 31

Strength

For the past few months, I've been going to the local fitness center to exercise and work out on the weight machines. It has really helped me, but you have to keep it balanced. I've noticed some people up there, that their arms look like tree trunks; they spend just about every day up there working out to build up strength. I've even noticed myself at times, looking in the mirror to see if I have improved any. In Proverbs 24:5 the Bible says, "A wise man is strong, yes, a man of knowledge increases strength." Psalm 105:4 says "Seek the Lord and His strength; seek His face evermore!" We need to exercise, eat the right foods; but if we are to pump iron – let's do it in the spirit and not in the flesh.

_____

_____

_____

_____

_____

August 1

Proclaimer Proclaim

Did you know as a Christian, people are looking at you? We have to be willing to turn our "proclaimer" on, the moment our button is pushed. Isaiah 61:1-2 says "The Spirit of the Lord is upon me, because He has anointed Me to preach good tidings to the poor, He has sent Me to heal the broken-hearted, to proclaim liberty to the captives, and the opening of the prison to those who are bound; to proclaim the accept-able year of the Lord..." Yes, turn your proclaimer on, and shine for Him - you may be the only Bible some people will ever see!

_____

_____

_____

_____

_____

August 2

Persecuted

The church of Jesus Christ is really going through persecution these days, but we can receive that in one of two ways. We can either backslide because of pressure; or be glorified for standing up and fighting the good fight of faith. Matthew 5:11-12 Jesus said, "Blessed are you when they revile and persecute you, and say all kinds of evil against you falsely for My sake. Rejoice and be exceedingly glad, for great is your reward in Heaven..." Just dwell on that verse when they come at you; take it as an opportunity to come back with some news about Jesus. Don't you give an inch; back the devil up, and make him wish he would have never opened his mouth. So when the persecution comes - don't backslide, and you will be glorified.

_____
_____
_____
_____
_____

August 3

Counterfeit

Did you know that when they teach bank tellers on counterfeit money, they never show them a counterfeit bill? They train on the good bills; when a phony comes along, they can pick it right out. In 1 John 4:1 the Bible says, "Beloved, do not believe every spirit, but test the spirits, whether they are of God; because many false prophets have gone out into the world." If you stay in prayer and read your Bible on a regular basis, you'll notice a counterfeit when they come by; something on the inside will say "counterfeit, counterfeit!" Stay focused in on the Real Thing - the Holy Spirit will show you the counterfeit.

_____

_____

_____

_____

_____

August 4

Man from the Station

Did you hear about the little boy who went to his mother with a stomachache? She said, "Oh honey, I'm sorry to hear that. Let's pray and ask Jesus to heal you." Well, they prayed together and in a little while the boy came back to his mother and said, "Mom it still hurts." She said, "Honey wait for the manifestation- it's coming." After awhile the little boy was back again and said, "Mom my stomach is still hurting, when did you say the man from the station was coming?" Jesus said, "He that has an ear, let them hear what the Spirit says unto the churches." There are beautiful truths in the Bible. We need to be compassionate, and ask God how to deliver these truths to a world that does not understand spiritual things. Don't give up church - manifestation is on the way!

_____
_____
_____
_____
_____

August 5

Use the Right Keys

Everyone has a set of keys; there is a key for your home, there is a key for your car. You cannot use the key for your home to start your car, and you cannot use the key for your car to open the door to your home. In Matthew 16:19 Jesus told Peter, "I will give you the keys of the Kingdom..." As a believer in Jesus Christ you have those same keys. If someone needs salvation, share with them the keys of salvation- so they can be unlocked from bondage. If someone needs physical healing, share with them the key from scriptures- that it is God's will for you to be well. Set them free through the key of healing - don't let the devil rob you of your keys!

August 6

Gifts

Do you receive gifts during your birthday or Christmas time? Doesn't it bless you when someone gives you a gift? My children get so excited when I bring gifts home; they want to know, "What's in the bag, Daddy?" Do you know that Jesus has given you gifts as a believer? When you heard the word preached, you received the gift of salvation. On the day of Pentecost, one hundred-twenty believers received the gift of the Holy Spirit, and spoke in tongues as the spirit gave them utterance. In 1 Corinthians 12 there are nine other gifts God wants to give you. Ask Him to fill you with the Spirit, so you can receive the gifts as you need - to minister to people.

_____

_____

_____

_____

_____

August 7

Stinky Fridge

My youngest daughter opened the refrigerator the other day, and she said, "It stinks in there, Mama." When my wife checked in to the problem, she found some water had drained down on the back shelf and had become stagnant. When she faced the problem, it sure did smell good again. In Psalm 19:9 the Bible says, "The fear of the Lord is clean, enduring forever." Check your heart, to see if anything is stinking to God. Let Him clean it up - so you can smell good for Him, and be the witness for Jesus that He wants you to be.
In Proverbs 23:19, the Bible says to keep our hearts on the right path.

_____

_____

_____

_____

_____

August 8

Hard Bread

Have you ever noticed how hard bread becomes, when it sits for a long period of time? Take that same bread, put it in the microwave, and it becomes so soft and warm. That's how we can get- if we sit around and gripe and complain. We become hard as that bread. In Isaiah 45:9 the Bible says, "Woe to him who strives with his Maker... Shall the clay say to him who forms it, what are you making?" When you notice your heart becoming hard, jump into God's microwave - and let Him make you soft, loving, and warm.

_____

_____

_____

_____

_____

August 9

No Trespassing

Have you ever noticed a no trespassing sign on someone's property? You may be able to walk there for a little while; but when the owner finds out that you are there without his permission, you might be looking at a double-barreled shotgun. Did you know the devil is like that? He comes on your property without permission- trying to put fear, doubt, and anxiety, and robs you of your joy. In Hebrews 10:35 the Bible says, "Therefore do not cast away your confidence, which has great reward." When you dwell on these lies, you cast away your confidence. Load your double-barreled shotgun with scriptures, and run the devil off your property - and shout the victory in the name of Jesus!

_____

_____

_____

_____

_____

August 10

Dessert

Can you imagine sitting down to your favorite dessert, and suddenly you realize the most important ingredient has been left out? The sweetness is missing. In Ezekiel 3:3-4 the Bible says, "Son of man, feed your belly, and fill your stomach with this scroll that I give you. So I ate, and it was in my mouth like honey in sweetness. Then He said to me, Son of man, go to the house of Israel and speak with My words to them." When we share Jesus, let's make sure our words are like honey; so that what we say will be received as a dessert - straight from Heaven.

_____

_____

_____

_____

_____

August 11

Aches and Pains

Can you imagine what it would be like to have a sure-fire cure for all your aches and pains? In the natural world, our minds say reach for the medicine cabinet; and find a pill that will cure the problem. Thank God for natural medicine; but do you know there is a spiritual medicine that has been on the market for years, and if taken regularly, you will be less dependent on natural medicine? In Psalm 103:3 the Bible says, "Who forgives all your iniquities, and who heals all your diseases." In Matthew 8:17 it says He carried our diseases; Jesus did it all. So next time aches and pains come, reach for the Word of God- which is your medicine cabinet. Tell the devil what the Bibles says in the name of Jesus - and watch him take off!

_____
_____
_____
_____
_____

August 12

Junk Food

Everywhere you go these days to eat, so many places are serving junk food. It tastes so good; but eat too much of this junk food, and your body sill start to have problems. In Psalm 119:103 the Bible says, "How sweet are Your words to my taste, sweeter than honey to my mouth." Your spirit needs the Bible each day, so it can grow strong. If you put gossip, strife, hatred, bitterness, envy, pride, MTV, soap operas, and other things in that go against God, this is junk food. We need the right foods to keep our body strong, and the right food to build up our spirit man. Eat your Word each day, and hang around strong Christians - the junk food of this world can give you heartburn!

_____

_____

_____

_____

_____

August 13

Washing Machine

Have you ever been around some people, and all they want to do is stir up strife? It's like you're listening to one big soap opera. In Proverbs 10:12 the Bible says, "Hatred stirs up strife, but love covers all sins." In Proverbs 10:23 it says, "To do evil is like sport to a fool..." They live every day just to grind away at you. They are just like washing machines; all they want to do is agitate. Christians are like washing machines, too; as we love and pray for them - they are put on the spin cycle!

_____
_____
_____
_____
_____

August 14

His Sight

Have you ever noticed on a clear day, how far you can see compared to a cloudy day? But still on a clear day, your vision is limited. In our walk with the Lord, we have a tendency to look with the natural eye and not with the spiritual eye. We determine our joy in the Lord by how we feel, rather than by what the Bible says. In 2 Corinthians 5:7 the Bible says, "We walk by faith, not by sight"; you can't see faith with the natural eye. We do not live according to the world's way. We are heavenly beings, heavenly minded, so our talk, walk, and everything we do is not of this world. If some people just can't understand you at times, you tell them you're not living by eyesight - but by His sight.

_____

_____

_____

_____

_____

August 15

Panic

Have you ever noticed before a major snow comes into the area, three or four days before it hits, people panic? They are at the grocery store buying everything out; they believed those weather reports, and prepared for it. If people could just believe what the Bible says about hell, and prepare for that. In Isaiah 14:9 the Bible says, "Hell from beneath is excited about you, to meet you at your coming..." In Psalm 55:15 it says, "Let death seize them; let them go down alive into hell." Let's continue to be God's weather man, telling the world that their future is going to be very warm - if they do not ask Jesus into their heart. He is our life insurance policy!

August 16

Worship

When you hear the word "worship", what does it really mean to you? In Vines" Expository Dictionary it says, "To worship is to do reverence, stressing the feeling of awe or devotion, and to honor." I used to have a dog when I was a kid; and when I came home from school he would jump all over me, licking me and wagging his tail. He was excited to see me. In Hebrews 4:16 the Bible says, "Let us therefore come boldly to the throne of grace, that we may obtain mercy and find grace to help in time of need." When you go into prayer and worship, don't let the devil rob you by reminding you of your sins. They are under the blood; worship Him in confidence. You will get excited, you may jump and dance before Him - because He is your Master, and He loves you so much.

August 17

Keeping Pouring It In

Have you ever taken a glass of dirty water and put it up to the light, and noticed how yucky it looks? If you keep running pure water in that dirty glass, in just a few minutes, it will be pure and clean. Proverbs 30:5 says, "Every word of God is pure..." If we put more Word in us, than world in us- we are pure before the world. They look at you and say, "You look so clean. How did you get like that?" It all started when you were born again; but you are responsible for coming under that heavenly faucet each day - and letting Jesus keep you pure and squeaky-clean!

August 18

Testify

I believe one of the greatest joys we have as believers, is the privilege of testifying of the Lord Jesus Christ; telling others over and over again that Jesus saves, and He loves them. In 1 John 4:14 the Bible says, "And we have seen and testify that the Father has sent the Son as Savior of the world." If every believer were doing this on a regular basis, the world would see that we mean business. In 1 John 4:20 it says, "If someone says „I love God" and hates his brother, he is a liar. For he who does not love his brother whom he has seen, how can he love God whom he has not seen?" In order to be a good testifier, you have to love your brother - so you will not become a "testi-liar"!

_____

_____

_____

_____

_____

August 19

Shortcut

I was coming home on the interstate a while back; the traffic was really backed up. The exit that I needed to get off was just about quarter of a mile ahead. Some people were using the shoulder or emergency lane, to get ahead of traffic. I thought, I'll take a shortcut; it's just a quarter of a mile. The Holy Spirit spoke inside of me and said, "You shouldn't do this." Well I pulled out and was on the shoulder, and there he was...a State Trooper parked in the emergency lane. I got back in the right lane real quick. In John 14:6 Jesus said, "... No one comes to the Father except through Me." There are no shortcuts to Heaven, Jesus is the only way. Keep telling the Good News- there are too many people on the shoulder of the road.

_____

_____

_____

_____

_____

August 20

Young People

I see a lot of young people in trouble today, and sometimes I wonder how it all started. There has to be a root cause. In Romans 1:30, the Bible speaks of children being disobedient to parents. Kids, the best way to keep the devil off your back is to obey your parents, even when it hurts. Luke 18:20 says, "...Honor thy father and thy mother." In Ephesians 6:4 it says, "Fathers, do not provoke your children to wrath..." I think the best way to get that child to be obedient is to spend time with them, hear the other side of the coin. Dad, if you have a bad attitude, ask the kid to forgive you; let's open our hearts to each other. The devil is out there ready to gobble your kids up. Parents, let's work on our end; kids, work on your end - and the devil will not get in!

_____

_____

_____

_____

_____

August 21

Be Patient

It is going to be a wonderful day when Jesus comes back, but the devil is doing everything he can to discourage the church. James 5:7-8 says "Therefore be patient, brethren, until the coming of the Lord. See how the farmer waits for the precious fruit of the earth, waiting patiently for it until it receives the early and latter rain. You also be patient. Establish your hearts, for the coming of the Lord is at hand." With the events taking place in Eastern Europe and the earthquakes, people are saying now we could have world peace. Jesus said these things would happen. Hallelujah, I'm excited; let's not drop the ball now, we're on the ninety-nine yard line. Time is running out, the devil knows it. We've already won - we just have to carry the ball across the goal.

August 22

Not Ashamed

Have you ever noticed some people when you get around them, all they talk about are their favorite basketball player, football team, and racecar driver? They know everything about the person and his team. They aren't ashamed of them at all. Romans 10:11 says, "Whosoever believeth on Him shall not be ashamed." Yes, we have someone to talk about, too. He is the greatest player of all time, and He has the best team on the face of this earth; I'm honored to be a member of this team. The next time you're around the sports enthusiast, don't forget to mention your favorite player who has the best record; He never lost a fight - and He is coming back for His team.

August 23

Being Free

Isn't it good to know that we are free in Jesus Christ? We do not need to walk around like we've been baptized in pickle juice. In Ezekiel 36:25-26 it says, "Then will I sprinkle clean water upon you, and you shall be clean; I will cleanse you from all your filthiness and from all your idols. I will give you a new heart..." Yes you are free, so be free; you're strong, so be strong. Now that you are a new creature, it's your nature to be free, happy, strong, loving, kind, and bubbling all over with the joy of Jesus. So get out of the pickle juice - and into the heavenly juice!

_____
_____
_____
_____
_____

August 24

Enemy Defeated

I read somewhere one time where two American Soldiers were in a battle with the enemy during World War II. All of their buddies had been killed except them. They put their backs to each other, and with their machine guns killed over a thousand of the enemy. In Joshua 23:10-11 the Bible says, "One man of you shall chase a thousand, for the Lord your God is He who fights for you, as He promised you. Therefore take careful heed to yourselves, that you love the Lord your God." We have to be aggressive in these latter days; stand your ground, and don't back up. When you have the Lord fighting for you, demons fall like bowling pins. So be of good cheer, saints - get back in prayer, and you will defeat your thousand and ten thousands!

_____

_____

_____

_____

_____

August 25

Divorce

The divorce rate is the same in the church as it is in the world; it should be our nature to love one another. In Matthew 19:5-6 Jesus said, "For this reason a man shall leave his father and mother and be joined to his wife, and the two shall become one flesh." If you are a Christian and willing to work on your marriage, God can restore it. It has to be both of you willing; drop that pride and say, "Honey, let's work on our relation-ship." Men, take your wife out to dinner, and look her in the eyes and tell her you love her. Ladies, stop complaining, and start telling him he's the best thing in your life other than Jesus. Divorce is not the answer.

_____

_____

_____

_____

_____

August 26

Endless Genealogies

I was talking to a man one time that was searching his family tree, and he was so excited about where he came from. He asked me was I interested in finding out my ancestors. I told him I was more interested in Jesus, where He came from and what He did for me on the cross. I'm a new creation in Christ, what difference does it make what color I am or where I came from? In 1 Timothy 1:4 the Bible says, "Nor give heed to fables and endless genealogies, which cause disputes rather than godly edification which is in faith." We are not of this world; you are not the same - but born new, through the precious blood of Jesus!

_____

_____

_____

_____

_____

August 27

Jesus Loves to Make House Calls

I remember as a child, our family doctor from time to time would make house calls when we became ill; he was such a loving and compassionate man. You don't hear of doctors today making house calls, but there is still one doctor that is making house calls; His name is Jesus. Psalm 50:15 says, "Call upon Me in the day of trouble; I will deliver you, and you shall glorify Me." Yes, Jesus is still making house calls. In Revelation 3:20, the Bible says that He's standing at your door knocking; if you open the door, He will come in. So call on the Doctor of all doctors - because He just loves to make house calls!

_____
_____
_____
_____
_____

August 28

Blah Monday

Have you ever noticed how people come to work on Mondays - all hung over and with the blahs? That's because they have been dwelling on the wrong things over the weekend. On the other hand, the Christian has gone to church on Sunday, and worshipped the Lord. He feels great on Monday, ready to go at it full steam. The world thinks you're crazy, acting like that on Monday; they think you should act like that on Friday. In Isaiah 38:19 the Bible says, "...the living man, he shall praise You, as I do this day..." That means Monday, and every day of the week. When Jesus comes back, it could be on a Monday; and I don't want Him to find me hung over - but taking over!

_____

_____

_____

_____

_____

August 29

How You Care

Have you ever run into people who are not interested in you, or what's happening in your life? All they are interested in is telling you how much they know. You never see them helping anyone out, but they love to talk about themselves. In Galatians 6:3 the Bible says, "For if anyone thinks himself to be something, when he is nothing, he deceives himself." Proverbs 21:24: "A proud and haughty man – "Scoffer☐ is his name; He acts with arrogant pride." When you receive knowledge from the Lord, put it to action after you have digested it and are walking it yourself. The more of the Bible we learn can hurt people, if not shared in the right spirit. People don't care how much you know – till they know how much you care.

_____
_____
_____
_____
_____

August 30

Radar Women

I would like to address the husbands and the wives in this warm-up. Genesis 2:24 says, "Therefore a man shall leave his father and mother and be joined to his wife, and they shall become one flesh." Wives are like radar; they pick up on things quick. If you are close to your wife in prayer and communication, she can be a great asset to you the husband, who is the warrior of the home. She can let you know of enemy attack that is coming. If you don't pay attention to the radar screen, and think you can do okay without it, you're in for a big attack on all sides. When anxiety sets in, she becomes fearful and nagging; that's a sign...there is trouble with the radar screen. Get back in prayer with her, communicate; listen to her as she expresses her problems, and both of you give it to Jesus. The radar will once again be back on track - and the warrior will know how to fight the enemy.

August 31

Flowing Zone

Has anyone or a group of people ever gotten you in a corner on such issues as, why do you have to be born again? Do you mean to tell me that I will go to hell if I don't repent? Why can't I be a homosexual and a Christian, too? I need to have a girlfriend on the side. Why isn't abortion okay? In 1 Corinthians 6:9-10, "Do you not know that the unrighteous will not inherit the kingdom of God? Do not be deceived." In summary, it goes on to say neither the sexually immoral, nor homosexual, nor thieves, nor the greedy. Let's not compromise with God's Word; we need to talk it straight, in a spirit of love. And get out the comfort zone - and into the flowing zone!

_____

_____

_____

_____

_____

September 1

Prayer Changes You

Did you know when you come to the Lord in prayer, and start praising Him for who He is; things not only change around you, but you change? In Philippians 2:5 the Bible says, "Let this mind be in you which was also in Christ Jesus." The more we pray on a consistent basis, the more of the mind of Christ we have. Then when we read the Bible, we receive more of an understanding of the scriptures; because we have spent time with the Father who wrote the book. Our ways are not God's ways. In Romans 8:6, it says for us to be spiritually minded and not worldly minded. Our thinking is different from the world; let's remember this the next time we pray. Allow the Holy Spirit to work in the areas of your life that need changing - then He will change the circumstances around you.

_____

_____

_____

_____

_____

September 2

Share the Word

When you meet someone for the first time, what is going through your mind about them? As a Christian, you will after a period of time be given the opportunity to stand up for Jesus, or deny Him. Our first concern should be, "Jesus, does this person know you as Savior?" In 2 Corinthians 5:18, the Bible says God has given us the ministry of reconciliation; so it's our main job to lead people to Jesus. We do this through prayer, living a clean life, and talking about Him. Since 1950, the world has doubled in population. The next time you meet someone, after the small talk - ask them do they know Jesus, it would be a matter of life and death!

_____
_____
_____
_____
_____

September 3

We Have Power

I run into people all the time that say, "Boy the devil really worked on me today. He did this, and he did that." I know they don't realize it, but they are just giving attention to him, rather than Jesus. In 1 Corinthians 15:57 the Bible says, "But thanks be to God, who gives us the victory, making us conquerors through our Lord Jesus Christ." We need to act like we are winners; the joy of the Lord is our strength. We need to talk like we are alive and not dead; people are watching us. The next time the devil gives you a hard time, don't tell the world what he's doing. Tell them how Jesus is helping you - to work out the problem.

_____

_____

_____

_____

_____

September 4

Helping Hand

Have you ever tried to move a piece of furniture, and it was just too heavy? Then you got on the phone and asked your neighbor for a helping hand. In Isaiah 41:10 the Bible says, "Fear not, for I am with you; be not dismayed, for I am your God. I will strengthen you, yes, I will help you, I will uphold you with My righteous right hand." I was getting discouraged when I couldn't move that furniture on my own strength, but when I called my neighbor it was such a relief. Our Father wants to give us a helping hand, but He can't unless we call on Him. Are you struggling trying to move something in your life? Call your neighbor, the Lord Jesus Christ. He will come over and strengthen you with His right hand. Back up devil - cause it's about to move!

September 5

Pleasing Him

Have you ever done something for someone, and it blessed them so much- that they would start to tell others what you did? When it got back to you, didn't it make you feel wonderful, how they were so pleased about that little thing you did for them? In Hebrews 11:6 the Bible says, "Without faith it is impossible to please Him..." If you have sickness in your body, please the Lord by acting on your faith. If you have trouble financially, please God by giving to Him by faith; and watch Him bless you because He loves you. We please Him by trusting Him to work it out; fear is faith in the devil. In Hebrews 10:35 it says, "Do not cast away your confidence, which has great reward." Let's please the Lord every day by acting on His Word. Then His Word will become flesh through our lives - and God the Father will be saying, I am sure pleased with you.

September 6

Earthquakes

I was talking with a group of people the other day, and they were talking about all the earthquakes that were reported in the newspaper. Since most of these people were unbelievers, it was a perfect time to tell them what was reported in tomorrow's newspaper, the Bible. In Revelation 16, the Bible talks of the seven bowls of wrath that are coming on the earth, at the end of the tribulation. The last of these bowls is the great earthquake recorded in verses 17-21. It will be the greatest of all earthquakes and level every mountain, then hailstones weighing one hundred pounds will fall from Heaven. I told them they could escape this terrible period of time that's coming, if they would ask Jesus to forgive them and be their Lord and Savior. We must use today's newspaper - as a door to talk about tomorrow's newspaper!

September 7

Be a Siren

I was talking to a man on the phone the other day, and in the background, his dogs were barking at a fire truck with its siren going off. That sounds exactly like the devil. In 1 Peter 5:8 the Bible says, "Be sober, be vigilant; because your adversary the devil walks about like a roaring lion, seeking whom he may devour." He barks at you because you are sounding off your siren for Jesus. He wants to shut you up by threats and loud barks, but you keep the siren up for Jesus. In Joel 2:1 it says, "Blow the trumpet in Zion, and sound an alarm in My holy mountain." Keep sounding the alarm for Jesus; when the devil is barking - that's a good sign our alarm is being heard.

_____

_____

_____

_____

_____

September 8

Murmuring

I was in my office one afternoon; it was pouring down rain. As I was studying, I noticed some water flowing down on the inside of the window. The next day, I took some caulking and fixed that leak. In 1 Corinthians 10:10, Paul referred to the Israelites when they were in the wilderness, that God turned them over to the destroyer because they were murmuring and complaining. When we murmur and complain, God can't protect us; the devil can have free access to any area of our life. It's only when we repent and pray for those that we've been talking about, that God comes with His Spirit- to fix the leak that has allowed the devil to enter in. Let's love one another in these latter days. When your roof starts to leak - fix it quick, with Jesus-stick!

September 9

Be as a Child

I went walking the other day with my youngest daughter and her friend, on a nature trail in the park. We came up to a little bridge, and there was a small creek running under the bridge. They took their shoes off and began to wade in the water. I was standing on the bridge and said to myself, I'm going to splash them. I took my shoes off, jumped off that bridge, and splashed them good. They just loved it, and were so surprised Daddy would do something like that. In Matthew 19:14 Jesus said, "Let the little children come to me, and do not forbid them..." Moms and Dads, let's not be so spiritual that we can't have fun with our children, so they can see Jesus in us.

_____
_____
_____
_____
_____

September 10

Old Lady

I was talking to a man the other day, and he was referring to his wife as "Old Lady". The Old Lady did this, and the Old Lady did that. I said, "Man, that is not your old lady." The Bible says when you find a wife, you find a good thing; it also says she is your crown. Tell her every day you love her, and she is the best thing in your life other than the Lord. In 1 Peter 3:7 it says, "Husbands, likewise, dwell with them with understanding, giving honor to the wife, as to the weaker vessel, and as being heirs together of the grace of life, that your prayers may not be hindered." Men, if we want our prayers to be answered, let's honor our wives; say good things to them and about them. Remember, they are our crown - not our old lady!

September 11

Blinded

I was talking to a man about Jesus one day, just telling him how good God is, and He will take care of you once you put your trust in Him. He said, "Jesus doesn't put clothes on my children's back." He then pulled a big wad of money out of his pocket and said, "This is what I trust in. This is my lord and savior." In 1 Timothy 6:10 the Bible says, "For the love of money is a root of all kinds of evil..." There is no U-Haul behind a Hurst. You can't buy enough suntan lotion to protect you in hell. Let's keep telling people about Jesus, so they can come to know the real peace and abundant life of Jesus Christ. I am wealthy - when I have Him.

_____
_____
_____
_____
_____

September 12

Storm

In Mark 4:38-39 the Bible says, "...They awoke Him and said to Him, "Teacher, do you not care that we are perishing?" Then He arose and rebuked the wind, and said to the sea, "Peace, be still!" So many people think that tornadoes and hurricanes are an act of God. The devil is the one that was trying to kill them in the boat, not God. The devil will try to kill you any way he can, if you do not realize the authority you have and rebuke it. Yes, I am saying if you are in a hurricane, tornado, or whatever, use your faith and come against that thing. It may seem impossible; but we must not look at the storm and fear- but in faith, and tell it to be still. What have you got to lose - try it sometime!

_____

_____

_____

_____

_____

September 13

Anger

Have you ever gotten angry at times? If you are human, then you have. You probably said something you wished you hadn't said. The lawnmower didn't start, and you kicked it and hurt your foot. Yes, I am confessing before the brethren. In Proverbs 16:32 the Bible says, "He who is slow to anger is better than the mighty, and he who rules his spirit than he who takes a city." That is a strong scripture. When the pressure is really on you, to be able to sing or quote a scripture is a good sign of maturity. It doesn't come overnight. Thank God for the pressure; because it gives us the opportunity to show others by our actions - that there is a greater One on the inside!

September 14

Trust

This is definitely the latter days that we are in; you have to really pray and forgive, just to keep your heart right. It's not the world that we Christians have problems with- it's those in the body of Christ that have wrong motives. In Matthew 24:10 Jesus said, "And then many will be offended, will betray one another, and will hate one another." It doesn't matter what people have done to you; stay in prayer, read your Bible, don't dwell on what they did to allow bitterness to creep in. Find you some good Christian friends you can trust. Love those that are giving you a hard time; let God work on them as you pray - and they'll soften up like jelly.

_____
_____
_____
_____
_____

September 15

No Coming Back

"For the Lord Himself will descend from heaven with a shout...And the dead in Christ will rise first. Then we who are alive shall be caught up together with them in the clouds to meet the Lord in the air...Therefore comfort one another with these words," 1 Thessalonians 4:16-18. I get excited when I read that; but I am at the same time burdened, because so many will be left behind. Church, tell people about Jesus every day; we don't want people to go to hell. Let's be faithful to that Great Commission; Jesus gave the job to us, we can do it. When you feel that fear coming on, share your faith - and it will leave as quickly as it came!

_____

_____

_____

_____

September 16

Open Mind

I was talking to a brother the other day on the subject of speaking in tongues, the Baptism of the Holy Spirit. I was telling him when praying in tongues, you are speaking to God and not to men (1 Corinthians 14:2). I told him as Christians, we needed to pray both ways, in tongues and with our mind, or English. In 1 Corinthians 14:14 Paul said, "If I pray in a tongue, my spirit prays." In verse 15 he says to pray with your spirit (or tongues), and with the understanding (or the mind). I asked the brother if he wanted to receive this; all you have to do is ask for it by faith. He said, "No, I heard it was wrong to do that." I told him you couldn't receive unless you believe; our minds are like a parachute - it only functions when it's open.

_____
_____
_____
_____
_____

September 17

Promises not Problems

In today's society, we think we have seen and heard it all; until we turn the news on, and there's something new that the devil has done. There are so many problems today; thank God through our Lord Jesus Christ, that we have the promises to overcome the problems. In Galatians 3:29 the Bible says, "And if you are Christ's, then you are Abraham's seed, and heirs according to the promise." We have the promise of salvation and healing for our bodies; the Lord wants us to prosper to be a good testimony for Him, and to bless others. Read over Deuteronomy chapter twenty-eight, and see the promises you have as a Christian. Your faith in God's Word will bring these things to pass. We have to let our light shine with the promises - to help those with the problems!

September 18

Joy

I am running into so many Christians that are unhappy; you can't be a testimony for Jesus if you're unhappy. In Acts 26:2 the Apostle Paul said, "I think myself happy, King Agrippa, because today I shall answer for myself before you concerning all the things of which I am accused by the Jews." Paul was ready to share about Jesus before the king. When you have souls on your mind, it makes you happy- because you are thinking of others, and not yourself. People will say things about you that aren't true, but stay happy; they will try to discourage you because you love Jesus, but stay happy. I want to be so full of the spirit of God, that if a mosquito was to bite me - he would fly away singing "There is Power in the Blood".

_____

_____

_____

_____

_____

September 19

Come Forth

Did you know when you got saved, it meant that you had eternal life and you're going to heaven? But until that time, He wants us to do something. In John 11:43, Jesus spoke to Lazarus after being dead four days and said, "Lazarus, come forth!" In verse 44 Jesus said, "Now loose him and let him go." When the Lord saved you, He said, "Come forth! Loose them, Devil, and let them go...to their families and friends and everyone my spirit leads them to...to say I am alive." I was blind, but now I see; Jesus raised Lazarus from the dead to testify of His power. Get all excited; go tell everybody - that Jesus Christ is King!

September 20

Keeping Out the Cold Air

When it's real cold in the wintertime, have you ever noticed around your doors and windows, the cold air that creeps through? Then when you had a chance, you put the proper insulation there to keep out the cold air. In 2 Thessalonians 3:6, Apostle Paul said, "But we command you, brethren, in the name of our Lord Jesus Christ, that you withdraw from every brother who walks disorderly and not according to the tradition which he received from us." If you have some friends that are busybodies and gossipers, wanting to cause strife all the time, you need to put the insulation up to keep that stuff out of your house. We have to stay away from this stuff in these latter days; or the cold air will come in - and the hot air will slowly leave.

September 21

Jumpstart

My battery went dead on my car awhile back, and I had to get a friend to jumpstart it for me. When that fresh current went to my dead battery, it fired right up. In James 5:19-20 the Bible says, "Brethren, if anyone among you wanders from the truth, and someone turns him back, let him know that he who turns a sinner from the error of his way will save a soul from death and cover a multitude of sins." If you see a brother hurting along the side of the road, pull over and offer to them a jumpstart. They have gotten lukewarm, and need that encouraging word. Be sensitive to those around you. When we plug up to God's current - it will jumpstart every dead situation!

September 22

Noisy Few

It is such a joy being a Christian in these latter days. When the devil sticks his head up on issues such as homosexuality, abortion, and wanting us to compromise with all kinds of sin; we should be ready to testify what the Word of God says. I do not mean getting into an argument; but just saying what the Bible says, and being willing to take the criticism. In Matthew 5:10 Jesus said, "Blessed are those who are persecuted for righteousness" sake, for theirs is the kingdom of heaven." The devil stands up for evil, and he's not ashamed. Why shouldn't we stand for Jesus and not be ashamed? God doesn't need a silent majority – He's looking for a noisy few.

_____

_____

_____

_____

_____

September 23

Lighthouse

There was a captain in the U. S. Navy who was in command of a battleship. One night he saw a light, which looked to him like another ship. They were headed straight for each other. The captain said, "Move 20 degrees to the right." A message came back, "No, you move 20 degrees to the right." The captain repeated his message. The same message came back, "No you move 20 degrees to the right." The captain replied, "I am a captain in the U. S. Navy on a battleship." A message came back, "I am a private first class in a lighthouse, and you had better move 20 degrees to the right." In Colossians 1:23 the Bible says to continue in the faith, grounded and steadfast, and to not be moved away from the gospel. Stand your ground; be a lighthouse - and you tell the devil to move!

_____
_____
_____
_____
_____

September 24

Preach Hope

There are so many people today messed up in dope; they are going to school on dope, on the job they're high on dope, while they are driving their car they are smoked up on dope. They are looking for that peace that can satisfy them; the things of the world just pull them further and further into bondage. There is no hope in dope. In 1 Peter 1:3 the Bible says, "Blessed be the God and Father of our Lord Jesus Christ, who according to His abundant mercy has begotten us again to a living hope through the resurrection of Jesus Christ from the dead." I am getting fed up with the devil preaching dope; we need to rise up and preach hope - to deliver them from dope.

_____
_____
_____
_____
_____

September 25

Backslide

We've got to get all excited, go tell everybody that Jesus Christ is King. I say, "Get all excited, go tell everybody, that Jesus Christ is King!" That's what we have to do, stay excited so we can go tell. That's how we backslide is when we lose that joy, that excitement. In 2 Peter 1:10 the Bible says, "Therefore, brethren, be even more diligent to make your calling and election sure, for if you do these things you will never stumble." When you know what God has called you to do, that will keep you from stumbling and losing your joy. We never "backdrop", we backslide; and that's a slow process. Witness every day for Jesus, bring them to your church, stay in your calling; and you will always be excited - to go tell everybody that Jesus Christ is King!

_____

_____

_____

_____

_____

September 26

When Pressured

What do you do when pressured by the world to do something you know is not right, but you do it anyway because you don't want all that hassle? I believe if we really search our hearts, all of us have been guilty of this at one time or another. But praise God for His love for us- that when we compromise we can come to Him, get it straight, and stand tall in the midst of all that persecution; and say "I am not backing up, devil." In Daniel 3:18, Shadrach, Meshach, and Abed-Nego said these words, "Be it known to you, O king, that we do not serve your gods, nor will we worship the gold image which you have set up." Let's not bow to the gods of this world; let them throw us in the fiery furnace - so they can see the power of the real God.

_____
_____
_____
_____
_____

September 27

Going Home

It is so easy sometimes to get discouraged. People are criticizing you because you're a Christian; they can't understand your motives. Every day it seems like a new level of persecution hits you, but we have to realize we are not of this world. In John 14:2 Jesus said, "In My Father's house are many mansions...I go to prepare a place for you." It's so exciting to read God's Word, and see the promises that await us in heaven. But through His love and promises, we can have heaven here on earth. Enjoy what the Lord has for you now. This will help when the trials come; they are opportunities to show forth God's power. Hang in there, Church - because it won't be long, we're going home!

_____

_____

_____

_____

_____

September 28

Family

Have you ever taken a family ride somewhere, and you know how to get there; but all of a sudden, they have ideas of a shortcut? I have two daughters, and my youngest said, "Go this way Dad, it's shorter." Well I went that way, and it wasn't shorter; but we learned a lot. One thing we learned is not to be double-minded. One would tell me, "this way Dad"; another would tell me "that way Dad." Well, they were doing their best, bless their hearts. In James 1:8, the Bible says a double-minded man is unstable in all his ways. If God is telling you to go in a certain direction in your life, be careful of all the voices around you. They may mean well - but you May wind up on the wrong road.

_____

_____

_____

_____

_____

September 29

Being Dead to Sin

Did you know when you got saved, you died? Your old man went into a coffin, and Jesus Christ nailed it shut by His blood. In Romans 6:6-7 the Bible says, "Knowing this, that our old man was crucified with Him, that the body of sin might be done away with, that we should no longer be slaves of sin. For he who has died has been freed from sin." Praise God, isn't that exciting? Your flesh wants to come out of that coffin from time to time and sin, but don't yield to it. The wind of the spirit is blowing; keep the old man in the coffin - nailed shut by the blood of the lamb!

_____

_____

_____

_____

_____

September 30

What Image are You

When you look in the mirror, what image do you see? Now I know you see your hair, nose, eyes, all that stuff, but what do you really see? In 1 Corinthians 15:49 the Bible says, "And as we have borne the image of the man of dust, we shall also bear the image of the heavenly Man." Do you see yourself as a failure- having doubt, unbelief, and fear- or do you see yourself in the image of the heavenly Man? Don't allow the devil to rob you of your image. See yourself as more than a conqueror in Jesus Christ; see yourself as a child of the King of kings and Lord of lords. Talk what you see to others, about Jesus" love; and you will be walking what you see. Have the image of the heavenly Man - Jesus Christ.

_____
_____
_____
_____
_____

October 1

Hear

Did you know that you hear what comes out of your mouth, before somebody else hears it? In Proverbs 18:21 the Bible says, "Death and life are in the power of the tongue, and those who love it will eat its fruit." If you are saying negative things all the time, cutting people down, complaining, and arguing with others, there is death coming out your mouth - to your ear and into your spirit. Speak life to others, and life will be in you. Encourage one another, it will help them to grow. We are people of life, not death; so let's get our mouth lined up with the Bible - and we will hear good stuff!

_____

_____

_____

_____

_____

October 2

Retired Sinners

I talked to a man the other day that said he was retired from his job; he wasn't going to work there anymore. That's what happened when we became Christians, we became retired sinners. We didn't work for the devil anymore. In Romans 6:22 the Bible says, "But now having been set free from sin, and having become slaves of God, you have your fruit to holiness, and the end, everlasting life." The devil wants you to come out of retirement and come back to work for him. Let's be a retired sinner, and not work for the devil anymore. I like my new employer, Jesus Christ - I am never going to retire from Him!

_____
_____
_____
_____
_____

October 3

What Goes Up

Have you ever noticed when you throw something up in the air, that eventually it will come down? That's the law of gravity; what goes up must come down. In Psalm 92:1 the Bible says, "It is good to give thanks to the Lord, and to sing praises to Your name." The joy of the Lord is your strength; you get strength by sending up praises each day. Tell Him how much you love Him, thank Him for what He has done for your life. He is our God, and He deserves our praises. Send the praise up - and the anointing will come down.

_____
_____
_____
_____
_____

October 4

Pit Bull

We have heard a lot about the Pit Bulls on TV and in news-papers lately. Those dogs are known for their strong jaws; when they bite something, they will not let go. As Christians, we need to be like a Pit Bull. You may have financial prob-lems; in 3 John 2 the Bible says, "Beloved, I pray that you may prosper in all things and be in health, just as your soul prospers." You bite into these scriptures until their blessing comes; don't give up. Are you sick? Bite into Matthew 8:17, and thank God for healing you until it comes to pass. Whatever problem we have, bite into it with the Word, and hang in there till it comes to pass. Be a Pit Bull Christian - and don't let go!

October 5

Hope Level

I was talking to a man the other day, and he said life just seemed so hopeless. He was a Christian, but his hope level was low. Proverbs 13:12 says, "Hope deferred makes the heart sick, but when the desire comes, it is a tree of life." Faith says you already have it; hope helps you to hang in there, until it comes to pass. Free yourself with God's Word; thank Him for what He has done, and what He is going to do. Don't let your heart become sick because of circumstances. In Proverbs 10:28 it says, "The hope of the righteous will be gladness..." Keep your heart clean before God - and you will always stay full of hope.

October 6

How Big is Your God

Have you ever found yourself telling people how big your problems are, instead of telling them how big your God is? Psalm 77:12 says, "I will also meditate on all Your work, and talk of Your deeds." When you meditate on who God is, and what He has done for you, He gets very big. If you are going through a crisis in your life and someone asks you about it, tell them how the Holy Spirit is helping you solve the problem. It is so exciting when we give God the glory by faith, when we don't see it. As we keep meditating on Him to work it out, and brag to others how big our God is; our problem gets smaller - because our God is bigger than the problem!

_____

_____

_____

_____

_____

October 7

Answer Man

Have you ever talked to someone who has all the answers, and everything you say they want to top it? They just have to get the last word in. Romans 12:16 (in the Amplified Bible) says, "Live in harmony with one another, do not be haughty or snobbish or high minded; but adjust yourself, and give yourself to humble tasks. Never overestimate yourself or be wise in your own conceits." Let's praise and uplift one another. In Proverbs 3:7 it says, "Do not be wise in your own eyes." Let's be very careful not to be haughty, but humble - so we won't grumble.

_____

_____

_____

_____

_____

October 8

Watermelon

Have you ever eaten a piece of watermelon, and noticed all the seeds in that watermelon? Did you know it only took one seed to get all of those other seeds? In Psalm 126:5-6 the Bible says, "Those who sow in tears shall reap in joy. He who continually goes forth weeping, bearing seed for sowing, shall doubtless come again with rejoicing, bringing his sheaves with him." At your place of employment, you may be the only seed. Keep sowing seeds of love, serving those that are against you, praying for them daily without doubting; but believing that one day, they to will come to a saving knowledge of the Lord Jesus Christ. In no time there will be a big, fat watermelon- full of seeds!

_____
_____
_____
_____
_____

October 9

Slurp on the Word

Every Saturday, my youngest daughter and I go to get a Slurpee. She loves to slurp all of it to the bottom of the cup. While I was driving home, I heard her going slurp, slurp, and slurp. I said, "Honey, you don't want to eat the cup." She just loves those Slurpees. In 1 Corinthians 10:4 the Bible says, "And all drank the same spiritual drink. For they drank of the spiritual Rock that followed them, and that Rock was Christ." This year, let's dedicate ourselves more to slurping more of His Word. Get that Bible out every free moment - and have a Heavenly Slurpee.

_____

_____

_____

_____

_____

October 10

You are Being Watched

Did you know that as a Christian, you are being watched? You're being watched at school, on the job, at home, church, and wherever you go; you're being watched. People are looking to you as an example, because you are God's representative on the earth. In Psalm 37:6 the Bible says, "He shall bring forth your righteousness as the light..." People are looking at you, because you are the light. That's when Jesus can really manifest His power through us, when the pressure is on. Don't compromise or back up; live godly before the wicked. They really want what you have, that's why they are watching you. Let the devil's KGB watch all they want; if they hang around us long enough – they'll defect to the outside!

_____
_____
_____
_____
_____

October 11

First Love

What is your motive for going to church, helping someone financially, sharing Jesus, and working in the church? What is your motive for doing godly work? In Revelation chapter 2, the Lord was proud of them for persevering, hard work; they were enduring for His name's sake and not growing weary. But He had one thing against them - they had lost their first love. When you do something for someone, it has to be because you love Jesus. If it's done for recognition or any other reason, God isn't going to honor that deed. We tithe because we love Him, we witness because we love Him, and we work in the church because we love Him. If we keep this in our hearts all the time - we will never leave our first love.

_____

_____

_____

_____

_____

October 12

Alive but Dead

Have you ever been around some people and even in some churches, they look like they are alive? They are saying and doing all the right things, but something isn't right. In Revelation chapter three, Jesus was speaking to the church at Sardis. He said, "I know your deeds that you have a name that you are alive, but you are dead." You may be thinking, how can that be? The people noticed the deeds of the church of Sardis and thought they were alive; but Jesus said, "They were dead," because they wanted to lift up self and not Jesus. He was telling them to repent and wake up; or He would come like a thief, and they would not know what hour. Let's make sure our deeds are alive and not dead. When the rapture takes place, I want to be alive and working for Him - and not asleep!

October 13

Stick Your Neck Out

God wants us to live by faith. In Hebrews 11:6 the Bible says, "Without faith it is impossible to please Him..." Faith is believing in what you do not see, faith is acting like it has already come to pass. Peter acted on faith, and he jumped out the boat and walked on water. Noah believed God for one hundred years building the ark, and it came to pass. By faith, the walls of Jericho fell down after they were encircled for seven days. By faith your husband or wife is going to get saved; by faith your healing is coming forth; by faith your financial needs will be met. By faith, God will give you strength to stand against those who oppose you. If you never stick your neck out – you'll never get your head above the crowd.

October 14

New Patch on Wineskin

When I was a kid growing up, I would always wear my pants out right on my knees. My mother would put a patch on them, but they stuck out like a sore thumb. After a while the patch would start to rip off from the old garment. Luke 5:36-37 says, "No one puts a piece of new garment on the old; otherwise it will tear the new, and they will not match. And no one puts new wine in old wineskins." If your church is criticizing you because you are born again or because you speak in tongues; and believe in divine healing and casting out devils - they still have the old garment on and the old wineskins. You need to ask God what you should do...

_____

_____

_____

_____

October 15

Clean Your House

What do you do before guests come to your house? I bet you have all the dishes washed, floors vacuumed, furniture dusted, grass cut; everything has got to look good. In Matthew 21:12-14 the Bible says Jesus entered the temple and cast out all those who were buying and selling in the temple, and said to them that His house shall be called a house of prayer. In verse fourteen, the blind and the lame came into the same temple, and He healed them. Isn't that wonderful? He cleaned the temple up, they sought the Lord through prayer, and then power went forth to heal those with problems. Let's be anxious to clean out our temple, seek God with all our heart; and when the guests come over - minister Jesus and set them free!

_____

_____

_____

_____

_____

October 16

Pride is Non-Fattening

There are all kinds of diets out today designed for you to lose weight. All of these companies say their method is the best. In Proverbs 16:18 the Bible says, "Pride goes before destruction..." Isn't this true when we overeat? We start to blossom in certain areas, then we feel ashamed because we weigh too much. After a while, destruction comes if we don't do something about it. Let's go on God's diet; swallow your pride – it's non-fattening.

_____

_____

_____

_____

_____

October 17

Sowing Seed

I saw a farmer sowing some seed one day as I was driving down the road. A few weeks later I came by, and the crop started to come up. The farmer had to do his part, before God could do his part. Mark 4:14 says, "The sower sows the Word." You are the sower; we have to sow before fruit comes forth. It might be on the wayside or stony ground, some are sown among thorns; but if you keep sowing, you will hit good ground. Saints, don't stop telling people about Jesus. Keep sowing the seeds; and believe God for the crop to come in, in due season. Remember Jesus came to destroy the works of the devil; the devil's works cannot be destroyed until you first sow the Word. Let's be farmers for Jesus - and expect a big crop!

_____

_____

_____

_____

_____

October 18

Double Agent

I was watching a spy movie one time, and they had a double agent in that movie that caused all kinds of problems. One day he was working for one country, and the next day he was working for the other country. That's how some church people are on Sunday morning. They will worship God and tell you how much they love Jesus; but during the week on the job, nobody knows they are Christians. When they are pressured by the world, they fold up and don't stand up for Jesus. When you say you are a Christian and don't live it, that's a double agent. Let's reach out to the double agents; and at the same time - be careful that we do not become one.

_____

_____

_____

_____

_____

October 19

Kangaroo Christian

Have you ever noticed a kangaroo with the baby in her pouch? The mother will let the baby out from time to time, to roam around; when the baby notices danger, he'll run back to mom and jump in the pouch. In Matthew 6:6 Jesus says, "When you pray, go into your room, and when you have shut your door, pray to your Father who is in the secret place; and your Father who sees in secret will reward you openly." Let's don't try to fight our battles on our own; let's go to the Father, jump up in His pouch, and He will take care of us. In Proverbs 30:5 it says, "He is a shield to those who put their trust in Him." Run to Big Daddy every day, jump in His pouch; put our trust in Him - and then He will shield us from the attacks of the devil!

October 20

Dark Times

I walked into a dark room the other night at my home. I couldn't see anything until I turned the light on. It ran all the darkness out. In Acts 16:25-26 the Bible says, "At midnight Paul and Silas were praying and singing hymns to God, and the prisoners were listening to them. Suddenly there was a great earthquake, so that the foundations of the prison were shaken; and immediately all the doors were opened and everyone's chains were loosed." Notice it was midnight- the darkest time. When they praised God and sang, then suddenly they were loosed. If it seems dark for you, keep praising God- because your "suddenly" is coming. Sing "The Joy of the Lord is your Strength"; turn on the light - by praising His wonderful Name.

_____
_____
_____
_____
_____

October 21

Tell Him Who You Are

Has the devil ever told you, that you are no good? "You can't really do the things you are trying to do for God. Nobody is noticing your work for God, so why don't you give up?" In Hebrews 6:10 the Bible says, "For God is not unjust to forget your work and labor of love which you have shown toward His name, in that you have ministered to the saints, and do minister." God sees your work, and that's all that counts. Tell the devil what God says about you and what you are doing. You have the power in you to do whatever God told you to do; if you didn't have it, He wouldn't have told you to do it. There are many souls out there to be saved. Don't let the devil talk you out of your confidence in Jesus Christ - we are more than conquerors through Him!

_____

_____

_____

_____

_____

October 22

Snooze Alarm

How many have a snooze alarm on your alarm clock? You might set it for 6:00 AM; it goes off, you push a button, and you snooze for fifteen more minutes. Has God's alarm ever gone off on the inside...for you to do something like, tell that person about Jesus... and you push the snooze alarm? Fifteen minutes later, it's too late. In Romans 10:14 the Bible says, "...How shall they hear without a preacher?" In 2 Timothy 4:2 it says, "Preach the Word! Be ready in season and out of season." When that alarm goes off for you to witness – don't push that snooze alarm.

_____

_____

_____

_____

_____

October 23

If There is a Will

I saw a bumper sticker the other day that said if there is a will, I want to be in it. I got so happy when I saw that; there is a will, and we can be in it. In Matthew 12:50 Jesus says, "For whoever does the will of My Father in heaven is My brother and sister and mother." In Luke 22:42 He said, "Father... not my will, but thy will be done." Don't be entangled by the things of this world; seek His will for your life - all of your needs will be met. Don't put your eyes on the worldly things; "seek ye first the kingdom, and all these things will be added unto you." It's fun to be in His will!

_____

_____

_____

_____

_____

October 24

Getting "Aids"

Did you know a Christian could get "aids" – acquired ignorance to the devil's schemes? In Proverbs 1:5 the Bible says,
"A wise man will hear and increase learning." When you
read God's Word daily, you increase learning and become
more aware of the devil's schemes. I know you don't want
to get "aids" [acquired ignorance to the devil's schemes]. So
eat on the Word - so you'll be ready for him when he attacks
with "aids". In 1 Peter 5:8 it says, "Be sober, be vigilant;
because your adversary the devil walks about like a roaring
lion, seeking whom he may devour."

_____

_____

_____

_____

_____

October 25

Can Dead Things Live

Have you had a hard time with certain areas of your life? Have you ever wondered if you'll ever get victory in that area? In Ezekiel 37, Ezekiel was in a valley of dry bones. God told him to speak to those dry bones; flesh came on them, then breath came into them, and they started to rattle. As he spoke, every time something happened. You have to speak to those dead areas of your life; tell them to come alive in Jesus" Name. Spend time in prayer and reading the Word; and before you know it, life will be there. You will start to rattle again, because you have spoken life into that dead situation.

Don't go by feelings - speak to the dry bones!

October 26

Change your Battery

I was at the jail the other day doing a Bible study, and when I came out I realized I left my lights on. My battery was dead, I mean graveyard dead. After a little push, I was able to get it started. We can't fight the devil on our own strength; I wouldn't push that car by myself, I needed some help. In Psalm 34:4 the Bible says, "I sought the Lord, and He heard me..." When you seek Him, He will hear you. When I looked for help that day, I found it; but if I would have sat in the car and not looked for help, I would probably still be there. If your spiritual battery is low, ask God for a charge or push. He'll come to your rescue - and you'll get the help you need.

_____
_____
_____
_____
_____

311

October 27

Dose of the Holy Ghost

Have you ever heard people say (and I've said it myself), when a cold or flu is coming on us, that we need to take a dose of this or a dose of that? It is a sure-fire cure for what ails you. TV commercials are flooded with cold remedies, but none of them ever mention the best medicine: it's called "Take a Dose of the Holy Ghost". In Proverbs 17:22 it says, "A merry heart does good, like medicine." Every day, take your daily medicine. Look up scriptures on healing, and eat them each day for your daily vitamins. Are you tired, and run because the devil has attacked you? Reach for the Word of God - take a big dose of the Holy Ghost!

_____

_____

_____

_____

_____

October 28

Adventures in Paradise

I'm sure that you have seen the ads in your newspaper, magazines, and on TV that say, "Come to the Bahamas, where you will find the peace you have been looking for; Take a seven-day cruise to Puerto Rico and find total peace." All of those things are nice, but let's take Jesus with us on the cruise. In Isaiah 26:3, the Bible says He will keep you in perfect peace, whose mind is stayed on Him. Our peace or relaxation is in Jesus; it's not the cruise to the Bahamas. It's not our new home, new car, job, clothes, or money. Our peace is in the Lord Jesus Christ; put Him first - and these things will fall into place.

_____
_____
_____
_____
_____

October 29

Christians Aren't Blue

What color is a Christian? There is one color that we should not be, and that is blue. I've seen so many Christians looking so blue lately. They look like they were just baptized in pickle juice, or have been eating lemons all day. We are the light of the world- we can't be blue; souls are at stake. Psalm 144:15 says, "...Happy are the people whose God is the Lord." We have to act like we are God's people, to draw them to a Savior that can deliver them from the blues. So the next time you are looking blue - turn to the one who can deliver you!

_____

_____

_____

_____

_____

October 30

Jesus is Our Standard

If you have your watch on your arm now, look to see what time you have. Do you know it's correct? How do you know it's the right time? What did you use as a standard? Most people call on the telephone to receive the correct time. But there is a standard the nation goes by to receive correct time; it's the Naval Observatory in Annapolis, Maryland. That's our standard. 1 John 4:1 says, "Beloved, do not believe every spirit, but test the spirits, whether they are of God; because many false prophets have gone out into the world." Let the Word of God be your standard; don't go by what other people tell you. Check it out - so you'll have the correct word all the time.

315

October 31

Head of Home

I would like to speak to the men in this Warm-Up. Are you the head of your home? I don't mean dictator; I mean head as in Ephesians 5:25, "Husbands, love your wives, just as Christ also loved the church and gave Himself for her." We don't need to remind our wives we are the head of the home. You serve them and love them, and you won't have a bit of trouble. That's why so many women are in rebellion these days; it's because the husband hasn't taken his rightful place in the home. Does your wife make all the decisions? It may be because you have backed up. Take your stand - help her out, serve her, and love her. Before long – you'll be the head again!

November 1

Submitting

I'd like to speak to the ladies in this Warm-Up. Ladies, the Bible says in Ephesians 5:24 "Therefore, just as the church is subject to Christ, so let the wives be to their own husbands in everything." That scripture pertains to everything in the Lord. If he asks you to do something that's wrong, against the Bible, you dig your heels in the carpet and say no. Pray for your husband, love him and serve him; but don't you let him put you in bondage. Yes, your husband is the head of the home, but you submit only in godly areas. It won't be long, and he will get the picture. We need more godly men in the church today - that are living what they are talking. The proof is in the home.

_____
_____
_____
_____
_____

November 2

Victorious

Did you know that you are victorious, no matter what condition you are in? In Romans 8:37 the Bible says, "Yet in all these things we are more than conquerors through Him who loved us." Whatever condition you are in, God says you are a conqueror. That's good news. In 1 John 5:4 it says, "Whatever is born of God overcomes the world. And this is the victory that has overcome the world – our faith." Don't look at the condition, but at the position; and that will make you a conqueror. Our faith overcomes the world. Use it on a daily basis, and your position will be constantly established on the solid rock - and that rock is Jesus Christ. Let's start acting like we are conquerors!

_____

_____

_____

_____

_____

November 3

Couch Potato

Have you ever heard of a couch potato? That's a person that sits around moaning, griping, and complaining all the time. They criticize everything that somebody is doing in the church. Everyone is wrong but them, yet they never tell anyone about Jesus or want to help in the church. They love their couch. In 2 Thessalonians 3:6 Paul said, "But we command you, brethren, in the name of our Lord Jesus Christ, that you withdraw from every brother who walks disorderly…" Hang around people who are burdened for souls and want to see the church built up. Stay away from the couch potato; if you aren't careful - you may find yourself a baked potato!

_____

_____

_____

_____

_____

November 4

Heat is On

There is heat on the body of Christ in these latter days, to deny Him and follow the ways of the world. Have you felt the heat? I sure have, and it's good for us. In Daniel 3:16-18, Shadrach, Meshach, and Abed-Nego would not bow to the pressure of the king to worship his god. They said to the king, "If that is the case, our God whom we serve is able to deliver us from the burning fiery furnace, and He will deliver us from your hand." Don't bow down and compromise. Stand up to the devil and say with your mouth, "I will not move one inch back; but every day go forward for Jesus - while the heat is on!"

November 5

Authority

I talked to a lady the other day that witnessed to a policeman; she reminded him that his position was ordained by God. In Romans 13:1 the Bible says, "Let every soul be subject to the governing authorities. For there is no authority except from God, and the authorities that exist are appointed by God." He said he wasn't a Christian, and she reminded him that he needed to turn his life over to Jesus, so he could be the officer God had called him to be. Let's pray for our governing authorities; and if God opens the door, share the love of Jesus with them because they have a lot of pressure on them. Remember they are working for you - not against you.

_____

_____

_____

_____

_____

November 6

Starting a Car

A friend of mine bought a new car the other day, and he said he had the hardest time figuring out the new gadgets. It wasn't until he looked at the owner's manual that he understood how everything worked. Have you ever wondered why some things just don't seem to work in your spiritual life? We have to keep reading our owner's manual, the Bible, to find out how it works. In Psalm 119:105 it says, "Your word is a lamp to my feet and a light to my path." If something isn't working, search and find out until the light from the Owner's Manual is shining on it - the Heavenly Owner's Manual is the only way to go!

November 7

Spirit of Esau

I have seen so many people lately that say they love Jesus, but what's coming out of their mouth is another story. We have to be careful of the spirit of Esau. In Genesis 25:33-34, it says Esau gave up his birthright for some stew and bread. The Bible says, "If you confess Him before men, He will confess you before the Father; if you deny Him, He will deny you." Don't turn your back on the one who didn't turn His back on you, but went all the way - by dying that you might live. Your salvation is more precious than anything in this world – let's let the world know it.

_____

_____

_____

_____

_____

November 8

Persecution

Did you know that persecution is a joy? In James 1:2 the Bible says, "Count it all joy when you fall into various trials, knowing that the testing of your faith produces patience." That's what the church is going through now. Use this time as an opportunity to share Jesus. In Matthew 5:10 it says, "Blessed are those who are persecuted for righteousness sake..." You know how you can tell you are living right before God? When the world is giving you a bad time, you say: Bring the persecution on, so I can share Jesus more. Did you know that persecution is an expression of the devil's terrible fear of us? Devil, you don't have a chance - as long as we stay under the blood of the Lamb!

_____
_____
_____
_____
_____

November 9

A Way of Escape

I talked to a brother the other day, and he said, "Hank, I have this sin in my life and I just can't overcome it. It haunts me all the time, and after a while I just yield to it." I'm sure all of us have gone through something like that at one time or another, but there is a way out. 1 Corinthians 10:13 says, "No temptation has overtaken you except such as is common to man; but God is faithful, who will not allow you to be tempted beyond what you are able, but with the temptation will also make the way of escape, that you may be able to bear it." When you are tempted by that sin, look for the way out; don't dwell on it. Jesus is the exit door - you have to love Him more than your sin.

_____
_____
_____
_____
_____

November 10

Lemon Life

Have you ever seen some Christians that seem like they have a lemon in their mouth all the time? ...The sourest-looking things you've ever seen. In Psalms 104:33-34 it says, "I will sing to the Lord as long as I live; I will sing praise to my God while I have my being. My meditation of Him shall be sweet; I will be glad in the Lord." That's why they look like lemons. We need to sing and praise the Lord. Thank Him for what He has done for us, and as you sing and praise, your meditation will be sweet. So the next time you feel a lemon has come in your mouth - meditate on Jesus and turn it into lemonade!

_____

_____

_____

_____

_____

November 11

The Gripers

Have you ever been around some people that love to gripe? They say, why isn't the church doing this, and why aren't they doing that. When the local church starts a building program, they are the first to gripe. When the young people want to do something, here comes the gripers, but they never volunteer to help. They are always there to give their two cents worth, but never their talents. In Isaiah 58:9-10, the Bible says, "If you take away the yoke from your midst, the pointing of the finger, and speaking wickedness...your light shall dawn in the darkness..." Givers never gripe - and the gripers never give.

_____
_____
_____
_____
_____

November 12

Pressure

Have you ever been to a junkyard and seen those wrecked cars crushed into a little box? Maybe you've seen it on TV or at the movies. In 2 Timothy 3:12-13 the Bible says, "All who desire to live godly in Christ Jesus will suffer persecution. But evil men and impostors will grow worse and worse, deceiving and being deceived." Yes, the devil wants to crush us and destroy our light. In Psalm 37:12-13 it says, "The wicked plots against the just, and gnashes at him with his teeth. The Lord laughs at him, for He sees that his day is coming." When the pressure is on, share Jesus and the devils will back up. They will try to put you in their crusher - but laugh at them in the joy of the Lord!

_____

_____

_____

_____

_____

November 13

Call on Jesus

It is so easy for us sometimes as Christians, when having difficulties such as sickness to call our doctor first. That's the first thing the world does. Now don't misunderstand me, I praise the Lord for doctors and the many accomplishments they have made. We have a family doctor ourselves, but I believe we as believers should go to the Lord first and apply our faith in that area. And if we need assistance from a doctor, don't get under condemnation, go to him. The Lord can work through him, too. In Hebrews 11:6 the Bible says without faith it is impossible to please God. So the next time you have a headache, take two prayers and call on Jesus -before you go to the medicine cabinet.

_____
_____
_____
_____
_____

November 14

Being Free

Did you know that when you got saved, God didn't want you to stop dancing, but just change partners? In Psalm 149:3 the Bible says, "Let them praise His name with the dance." There is something about dancing in His presence, but it's in the spirit and not in the flesh. Try it, it will set you free. There's nothing wrong with drinking. I didn't stop drinking when I got saved, I just changed brands. In Ephesians 5:18 it says, "Do not be drunk with wine...but be filled with the Spirit." I love drinking the new wine; it's been on the market about two thousand years. So don't stop dancing, just change partners; don't stop drinking, just change brands. There is never a hangover - off the stuff we're drinking!

November 15

Felt like Quitting

Have you ever felt like quitting at times? You love Jesus with all your heart, but because of so much immorality, drugs, violence, and people coming at you for no reason...well hang in there, church, there is good news. Hebrews 10:22-23 says, "Let us draw near with a true heart in full assurance of faith, having our hearts sprinkled from an evil conscience and our bodies washed with pure water. Let us hold fast the confession of our hope without wavering, for He who promised is faithful." If you haven't quit, you're winning; stay in there and fight. Remember - the devil has no teeth, just loud barks.

_____
_____
_____
_____
_____

November 16

Joy is Full

I was at the gas station the other day filling my tank up. Well, I wasn't paying much attention to what I was doing, and ran the gas over the top, onto my hand. It was full. In John 15:11 the Bible says, "These things I have spoken to you, that My joy may remain in you, and that your joy may be full." We need to stay full of joy. Let your joy run over to someone, like that gas did on my hand. Keep your heart right; pray in the spirit and with your mind. Read the heavenly newspaper each day to stay full. One thing was true about that gas tank; I couldn't get anything else in it. If you stay full of joy - there is no room for the devil!

_____

_____

_____

_____

November 17

Working Hard

Have you noticed lately that so many people are working so hard to go to hell? Just look around you. Most of them do not have time when you share Jesus. They are in such a hurry to get away from you. They just don't want to face the music. In 2 Peter 3:10-11 the Bible says, "The day of the Lord will come as a thief in the night... and the elements will melt with fervent heat; both the earth and the works that are in it will be burned up. Therefore, since all these things will be dissolved, what manner of persons ought you to be in holy conduct and godliness..." Don't give up saints, hang in there. Keep the fire of Jesus burning in your heart - our King is coming soon. The world is depending on us - we are all they have to show Jesus.

November 18

Grace

There is only one word for grace, and that is "amazing." I love Him so much I could pop sometimes. In John 1:17 the Bible says, "The law was given through Moses, but grace and truth came through Jesus Christ." The word "grace" means to delight, a pleasure, or favorable regard, loving-kindness. It was a pleasure in God's eyes to send Jesus to us. He delighted in doing that for us. Doesn't that make you happy? Let's dwell on what He did for us, we are His delight. He shows us loving-kindness; He is pleased with us for not giving up. When you break it all down, there is only one word for grace - and that is amazing grace!

_____

_____

_____

_____

_____

November 19

Upper-taker

If you talk to the average person today, they will most likely tell you that they have a will, have bought their burial plot, and are all ready for the undertaker; but they aren't that excited about the "upper-taker". In 1 Thessalonians 4:16-18, Paul said, "the Lord Himself will descend from heaven with a shout... And the dead in Christ will rise first. Then we who are alive and remain shall be caught up together with them in the clouds to meet the Lord in the air... Therefore comfort one another with these words." We are supposed to share the upper-taker; get people ready. The undertaker will surely get your body when you die, but without Jesus you will never get to the upper-taker. I'm looking forward to that great day - when the upper-taker says, "Come on home."

_____
_____
_____
_____
_____

November 20

Drunks in Church

Have you ever noticed people when they get drunk? They just seem to be so happy and could care less what people think; they are just having fun. Now we in the church have been delivered from that type of drinking, but why can't we get drunk in church off the new wine? Ephesians 5:18 says, "Do not be drunk with wine...but be filled with the Spirit." Have you ever noticed some when they get to raising their hands and dancing before the Lord, others will look at them and think they are out of their mind? No - they are just drunk and having fun, and getting high in the Most High!

_____

_____

_____

_____

_____

November 21

Vision and Division

Have you ever been in a church, and you just don't feel real peaceful on the inside? Your head agrees with what's going on, but for some reason you just don't feel right. It could be that you are in the wrong place. God sends certain believers to certain churches, to assist the pastor in the vision God has given him. There is nothing wrong with you feeling this way. In Exodus 18:25, Moses chose able men and made them heads over the people. All of these men had to agree with the vision God gave Moses, or there would be problems. You have to submit to that authority there and help them. If you can't, find somewhere that you can assist that man of God in his vision - or you will have division.

_____

_____

_____

_____

_____

November 22

Pit Bull Faith

I'm sure you have heard of a dog called a Pit Bull. Once they lock on to something, they don't let go. A man told me one time, a friend of his had a Pit Bull in a fenced-in yard. The dog was trained never to go outside of that fence. One day a neighbor's dog stuck his head through the fence. That Pit Bull caught him behind the neck and just held on. The neighbor tried to break him loose from his hook, but couldn't; the Pit Bull held on. In Hebrews 10:23 the Bible says, "Let us hold fast the confession of our hope without wavering..."
We need to use Pit Bull faith; hold on until your opponent is defeated - and victory will be yours!

November 23

An Excuse

Have you ever asked someone to do something for you, and they would always give you an excuse to why they couldn't do it? Deep down they just didn't want to do it for you, but just can't tell the truth, so they put you off. In Colossians 3:23, the Bible says, "And whatever you do, do it heartily, as to the Lord and not to men." If someone asks you to do something in the church, pray about it and do what God tells you to do. An excuse is a reason - dressed in a lie.

_____

_____

_____

_____

_____

November 24

Burden for Souls

We have such a wonderful God; He knows just what to do to meet every one of our needs. God saved us, not just to go to heaven; but that we would tell the world about the love of Jesus. Most Christians do not share Jesus because they do not have a revelation of hell. In Isaiah 14:9-11, the Bible says that hell is excited to meet you at your coming, and worms and maggots are your covering. Satan gets excited when you don't witness; he gets mad when you do. I like to make him mad; an attitude of prayer with a revelation of hell - will give you a burden for souls!

_____

_____

_____

_____

_____

November 25

Heavenly Security

Have you noticed how so many people put their security on decisions made in the White House? If things are fine, they are fine; if it's shaky, they get shaky. In Joshua 24:15, he made a decision. He decided as far as he was concerned, he was serving the Lord and everyone in his house, "As for me and my house, we will serve the Lord." The White House can say abortion is legal, men can live with men, women with women; but "as for me and my house, we will serve the Lord." Stand up, Church, don't back down. The decisions are coming; choose this day - whom you will serve.

_____

_____

_____

_____

_____

November 26

Flu and Healing Season

Have you ever had people say this is flu season, you had better watch out? I say, I'm in the healing season. When they talk about flu season, I talk about healing season. They look at you so funny. In Galatians 3:13, the Bible says Christ redeemed us from the curse of the law. We don't have to accept a flu season. The world needs to hear our talk, the heavenly talk of healing season. Can you imagine going into a crowd of people at work and saying, "Get ready, the healing season is coming!" All you have to do is believe that Jesus died for you; ask Him to forgive you - and the healing season is here!

_____

_____

_____

_____

_____

November 27

Firmly Rooted

Did you know that 90% of the adult population in the U.S. has periodontal disease? It is a disease of the gums that is caused by not cleaning our teeth properly. If not treated soon, our gums get soft and our teeth will eventually fall out, because our gums have become weak. In Colossians 2:6-7 the Bible says, "As you therefore have received Christ Jesus the Lord, so walk in Him, rooted and built up in Him and established in the faith, as you have been taught, abounding in it with thanksgiving." We need to keep our hearts clean; stay rooted in Jesus, so that we do not get infected by the disease of the devil. Use your Holy Ghost Water-Pick on a regular basis - and you will not get soft or weak.

_____
_____
_____
_____
_____

November 28

Giving

Have you ever had sinners to criticize you, because you tithe your income? I just love it when they open their big fat mouth, because I love to put scriptures in it. In Malachi 3:10-11 the Bible says to bring all the tithes into the storehouse, and the Lord will rebuke the devourer for your sake; so he will not destroy the fruit of your ground. I tell them they are tithing to their god, why can't I tithe to mine? The things they are investing in, such as drugs, alcohol, pornography, are bringing them death. The things we are investing in, such as souls for the kingdom of God, are bringing us life and joy - the best dividend we can ever receive!

November 29

Make up Quick

Men have you ever gotten angry with your wife? You just knew that you were right in that situation, and you were not going to give in. If you're not careful, the hours go by and you're not speaking to each other. She is saying in her heart, "I'm not giving in"; and you're saying the same thing. It is a seed of bitterness that we have allowed to enter in. In Ephesians 5:25 the Bible says, "Husbands, lover your wives, just as Christ also loved the church and gave Himself for her." Ask your wife to forgive you, whether you feel like it or not; and you will notice the love of Jesus going all over you, your wife, children, and every area of the home. The devil is defeated - because we're walking in love.

_____
_____
_____
_____
_____

November 30

Pray

Have you ever gone into prayer before the Lord feeling so awkward and wondering, "Father, where are You?" It seems as if He's a million miles away. If we aren't careful, we'll let the flesh get the best of us and not seek Him regularly. Jeremiah 29:11-13 says, "For I know the thoughts that I think toward you, says the Lord, thoughts of peace and not of evil, to give you a future and a hope. Then you will call upon Me and go and pray to Me, and I will listen to you. And you will seek Me and find Me, when you search for Me with all your heart." When we seek Him, that love that He shows toward us will flow to others - who do not know Him.

December 1

Haven't Got Time for the Pain

(Singing) "I haven't got time for the pain, for I'm healed in Jesus name," hallelujah! You know that's exactly what the devil wants to do. He wants to rob you of your time by hitting you with pain. In Matthew 8:17, "He Himself [meaning Jesus] took our infirmities and bore our sicknesses." Isn't that exciting? Doesn't that bless your socks off to know that He not only died for your sins, but also took away your sicknesses? So the next time the devil attacks you with pain, you tell him: I haven't got time for the pain – I'm healed in Jesus name. Oh, Hallelujah!

December 2

Don't Need the Dishwasher

When we moved into our first home, we didn't have an automatic dishwasher. After a while we started hearing about how nice they were, but we didn't think we needed one. A few years later we moved into our second home, and it had an automatic dishwasher. My wife said, "Honey, this thing is wonderful, where have we been all these years?" There are some Christians, bless their hearts, that think they don't need the baptism in the Holy Spirit with the evidence of speaking in other tongues. In 1 Corinthians 14:4, the Bible says tongues edify you. So ask Jesus for the gift of the Holy Spirit according to Acts 10:44-46. Then I know that you will say - where have I been all these years?

_____

_____

_____

_____

_____

December 3

Advertise His Name

I was driving down the highway the other day, and I noticed all the businesses, how they had their names proudly advertised for everyone to see. They want people to see their name and come in to buy their product. Acts 4:12 says "Nor is there salvation in any other, for there is no other name under heaven given among men by which we must be saved." We have to advertise that Name, it's the mighty name of Jesus. So advertise Him wherever you go, letting His light shine - to draw people in!

_____

_____

_____

_____

_____

December 4

Speak to the Mountain

Have you ever noticed how big and tall our mountains are, in the western part of the state? Sometimes circumstances and problems we run into can seem bigger than the mountains. In Matthew 17:20 Jesus said, "If you have faith as a mustard seed, you will say to this mountain „Move from here to there," and it will move; and nothing will seem impossible." Did you notice that Jesus said we have to speak to it? Proverbs 18:21 says, "Death and life are in the power of the tongue." If you want life in that situation, speak to it and tell it to move; be patient, stand on the word - and it will move.

_____

_____

_____

_____

_____

December 5

Tree of Righteousness

Did you know that you are a tree? You are a tree of righteousness according to Isaiah 61:1-3, the Spirit of the Lord is upon us to proclaim good tidings to the poor, to heal the brokenhearted, to proclaim the acceptable year of the Lord; we are to comfort those who mourn, set them free who are bound with evil spirits. Then we will be called trees of righteousness, the planting of the Lord, that He may be glorified. So you have within you righteousness; so get out there - and be a tree for someone who needs some shade!

_____

_____
_____
_____
_____

December 6

Holding On

Have you ever been around some people that just can't stand you? Everything you say they want to give you a hard time, because you love Jesus and are standing for righteousness. Sometimes you feel as if you want to take matters in your own hands. Jesus said, "Vengeance is mine, I will repay." In Revelation 6:10, the saints cried out and said, "How long, O Lord...until you judge and avenge our blood on those who dwell on the earth?" We've got to hold on and be patient; Jesus will work it out. He knows what you're going through. Keep praying for your enemies, this will keep love in your heart. It won't be long, saints – Satan's time is running out.

December 7

Up All Night

It is so easy to hold onto your problems. We nurse them so much they become part of us, and God doesn't want us to live like that. It's depressing and besides, nobody wants to hear you keep repeating them. 1 Peter 5:7 says, "Casting all your care upon Him, for He cares for you." You were not made by God to carry those problems. It will affect you mentally and physically. When you go to bed tonight, give those cares to the Lord – He'll be up all night!

_____
_____
_____
_____
_____

December 8

Leaving Heaven

Have you ever been around Christians who are always talking about the problems with their family, problems at work, and problems at church? It's like they are helping the problem get bigger by spending so much time on it; but when it's time for prayer at church, these people never show up. They are always saying they never have time to pray that much, because they're so busy. In Matthew 18:18, Jesus said if you bind anything on earth, it will be bound in heaven; if you loose anything, it will be loosed in heaven.
Nothing leaves heaven - until prayer leaves earth.

_____
_____
_____
_____
_____

December 9

Being Free

My wife Patsie was in the kitchen one day, and a cricket ran across the room. Well, you would have thought it was a snake or something in the house. She didn't care who was in that kitchen looking at her, going bananas. She was going to get that cricket out of her kitchen. In Galatians 5:1 the Bible says, "Stand fast therefore in the liberty by which Christ has made us free, and do not be entangled again with a yoke of bondage." That's the way Jesus wants us to be all the time; don't be concerned about people looking at you when God tells you to do something - go after it like Patsie went after that cricket!

_____
_____
_____
_____
_____

December 10

Draft Dodgers

I am a Vietnam Veteran, and during that time we couldn't understand why some people chose to be draft dodgers. They were running away from the battle. When we asked Jesus into our hearts, He called us to battle the enemy. In 1 John 3:8 the Bible says, "...the son of God was manifested, that He might destroy the works of the devil." Every time we win a soul for Christ, that's another soldier for the army. In John 14:12, Jesus said you can do greater works than I, because I go to be with the Father. He preached the gospel, healed the sick, cast out demons, and raised the dead. Let's have more faith in the Bible and less in the newspaper; don't be a draft dodger - fight the good fight of faith!

_____

_____

_____

_____

_____

December 11

Bubblegum

I remember when I was a kid playing baseball; we would take two or three pieces of bubblegum, put it in our mouths, and make big bubbles. Sometimes they would stick to our faces, and we had the hardest time getting that stuff off. Jesus wants us to stick to Him like bubblegum. In Proverbs 18:24 the Bible says, "...but there is a friend that sticks closer than a brother." We need to stick to Jesus, so people can see Him all over our faces like that bubblegum. When Jesus is shining on your face, don't try to pull Him off like the bubblegum - let Him stick on and on.

_____
_____
_____
_____
_____

December 12

Fly-Swatter

Have you ever been trying to take a nap, and a fly keeps buzzing around your head and just nagging you, to the point that you just have to get up and get that fly-swatter out? And all of your attention for the next few minutes is focused on "Operation Fly". You won't be able to rest until that fly is disposed of. That's the way Jesus wants us to fight the devil. In Mark 16:17, He says in My name you can cast out demons. They want to nag you and buzz around your head, to cause trouble in the home or wherever you are. Take authority over the situation; get your Holy Ghost fly-swatter out - and run him away in the name of Jesus!

December 13

Jackhammer

Have you ever noticed a man running a jackhammer? That thing is cutting on that concrete, until it breaks through to the soft ground beneath. When you share Jesus with some people, it's like coming up against concrete; but your prayers keep the jackhammer going. Your prayers are stronger than concrete, they can break through. Psalm 126:5 says, "Those who sow in tears shall reap in joy." Sow your seed, water it with prayer. Don't be weary in well-doing, and it won't be long; you'll be breaking through to that soft ground, and that person will open up and receive Jesus. Keep your jackhammer running; don't let the concrete bother you - because you have the Greater One inside!

_____

_____
_____
_____
_____
_____

December 14

Laser Beam

We have heard a lot about laser beams the last few years. They are able to cut through steel, transmit, and communicate. What impresses me about a laser beam is if you set it on a mark or destination, it will get there unless something that's stronger gets in its way. In Philippians 3:14, the Apostle Paul said, "I press toward the mark for the prize of the high calling of God in Christ Jesus." Don't let the devil get in your way, press on. He will try to stop you from reaching your mark, but let your laser beam shine. It's powerful and can burn through anything the devil puts in your path. He can't stand it when you're living a clean, holy life before God; keep it up saints - and you will reach the mark.

December 15

Camping Out

Have you every wondered why so many people that say they are born-again and love Jesus, yet you don't see fruit in their lives? They go to church every Sunday, but something is wrong. It's because they have been camping out too long. It's good to come into the camp and rest and get refreshed, but we can't stay there. In Joshua 6 the Bible says it came to pass on the seventh day, that they rose early and marched around the city; the priests blew the trumpet, the people shouted, and the walls came down. If they would have stayed in camp, the walls would not come down. Do you have some walls? Come out of camp - command them to come down in Jesus" name!

_____
_____
_____
_____
_____

December 16

Faith

What do we want to do more than anything else as children of God? Our desire should be to please the Father. In Hebrews 11:6 the Bible says, "But without faith it is impossible to please Him." When you acted on faith and got saved, that pleased the Father. When you asked by faith for the mighty Baptism in the Holy Spirit with the evidence of speaking in tongues, that pleased the Father. When the devil attacks you through sickness, and you apply your faith in Jesus" name, that pleases the Father. When you are persecuted for His name's sake and stand up for Him, that pleases the Father. When you put your hand to the plow and don't look back, that pleases the Father. Let's keep pleasing the Father by acting on the Word; faith is forsaking all - and trusting in Him.

December 17

Termite Control

The other day the termite man came by to inspect my house. After approving my home, we started to talk of the dangers of termites. You never notice they are there until a part of your house falls away. I started telling him that sin in my life years ago, was eating away at me; and it had almost destroyed me, until I invited Jesus Christ into my heart. He ran those devil termites out of my life. The blood of Jesus is our protection. Is sin eating away at you? In Psalm 51:2 David said, "Cleanse me from my sin." The termite man didn't come until I called; get on the hotline to heaven and call Jesus, the cleansing man – He'll make you free again!

December 18

Popcorn Christian

I wonder how many of you like popcorn. Just about every Saturday night in our home, we fix a big bowl of it. I think you've noticed that popcorn has to get hot before it pops. It can't be lukewarm, it has to be hot. In Psalm 39:3 the Bible says, "My heart was hot within me; while I was meditating, the fire burned. Then I spoke with my tongue." You can't speak the word of God and be effective for Him without your heart being hot. Our heart becomes hot when we meditate on Him; then the fire burns, and we speak with power. Let's dive into His bowl, allowing God to saturate us with the hot oil of His Spirit. It won't be long, and you'll be popping forth all over the place - winning souls for Jesus.

December 19

Bible Wearing Out

Is your Bible wearing out? It is a good sign that you are well put- together. In 2 Timothy 2:15 the Bible says, "Be diligent to present yourself approved to God, a worker who does not need to be ashamed, rightly dividing the word of truth." If you have a Bible you can't mark in or make notes, then give it away and get one you can mark in. If your Bible is wearing on the edges and the pages are tearing, it's a good sign you are well put-together in Christ. The devil doesn't like for your Bible to wear out; he wants it to lie around and collect dust. Let's give him a hard time - by wearing our Bible out!

_____

_____

_____

_____

_____

December 20

There is no High like the Most High

I run into people all the time that tell me, "There is no high like a cocaine high." They brag about alcohol and marijuana making them feel good. I usually tell them that Jesus is the real high. If they tried Him, they wouldn't go back to the stuff that's killing them. In Romans 6:23 the Bible says, "For the wages of sin is death, but the gift of God is eternal life in Christ Jesus." When they get high on the devil's stuff, he pays them back through hangovers, ulcers, and nervous breakdowns. It eats your whole body up, and they say it's fun; the next time they offer it to you - tell them there is no high like the Most High!

December 21

Christians on the Offense

Have you ever watched a football game and noticed that most of their points are gained on offense, while they have the ball? Very seldom do they get points on defense. In Proverbs 11:30, the Bible says he who wins souls is wise. You'll never win anyone to Jesus on defense; you have to have the ball. Stand up for Christ when they come at you. Whatever they want to talk about, don't back up; tell them what the Bible says. If they say to you, are you one those Christians? You say to them, are you one of those sinners? Stay on the offense. Pray for them to open the doors, and then you jump in and win that soul. The devil has lost another one - because we have the ball!

December 22

Divine Healing

Have you ever heard anyone say that divine healing is not for today? It was done away with when the last apostles died; if God wants you healed, He'll do it if it's His will. Well, the Bible says in Matthew 8:17 that He took away your infirmities and carried away your diseases. Now that is physical. In Hebrews 13:8 it says, "Jesus is the same yesterday, today, and forever." Divine healing and salvation is all one package. When people tell me that healing is not for today, I ask them, why do they go to the hospital? The devil doesn't want them to get better. Praise God for His Word, the doctors, and any group that's trying to help people with those problems.

_____

_____

_____

_____

_____

December 23

Oil Filter

Have you ever witnessed to someone about Jesus and they've said, "Well, I don't do the things I used to. I'm a better person now than a few years ago." In Ephesians 2:8-9, the Bible says we are saved by grace through faith, not works. I asked him did he ever try cleaning an oil filter. There will always be little specks of dirt, no matter how much you clean; you throw it away and get another one. In 2 Corinthians 5:17, it says the old is passed away, and all becomes new. He finally realized that is was only the blood of Jesus that could clean him up, and keep the little specks of dirt out of his life. Praise God for the blood of Jesus that keeps us continually clean - so our engine can run smooth!

_____
_____
_____
_____
_____

December 24

Jesus the Superman

He is able to leap over tall buildings at a single bound, faster than a speeding bullet, look up in the air! It's a bird, it's a plane, no – it's Superman! We heard a lot of talk about this man over the years, but there is One that is greater than Superman, and He isn't a make- believe character. He walked on water, rebuked the storms, and turned water into wine; healed the sick, cast out demons, and raised the dead. He replaced sorrow for joy, by dying for us on the cross and defeating the devil; His name is Jesus Christ - and He wants you to go forth with power!

December 25

Christmas Xmas

Have you ever noticed some people abbreviate the word Christmas and put Xmas? Now how can they say our Lord and Savior was an X? The word Christ means anointed. When you were born again, you were anointed with the Holy Spirit to preach Jesus. You were not known as an X; you are a Christian, or anointed one. That's just like the devil, to take a beautiful word like Christmas and make an X out of it. When I look at the letter X, it reminds me of used to be, past tense. Now as far as I am concerned, the devil is the X. In Revelation 19:20 the Bible says, "Then the beast was captured, and with him the false prophet... These two were cast alive into the lake of fire burning with brimstone." Now when I read that, it tells me the devil will be the X - or past tense, used to be!

December 26

Handcuffs

I saw a man a few weeks ago being escorted into a car. He was bound hand and foot, with handcuffs and chains on his feet. I thought that must be miserable. We as Christians can become bound like that, by things in the world, if we're not careful. In Hebrews 12:1 the Bible says, "Let us lay aside every weight, and the sin which so easily ensnares us, and let us run with endurance the race that is set before us." You can do nothing for God if sin is in your life; you want to be free and powerful for Jesus, just confess it to Him. The handcuffs will be torn off; the chains will not hold you back - because Jesus has set you free.

December 27

Turbo

I was going down the interstate the other day, and this car
passed me like I was sitting still. I thought, what has he got
under that hood? Well, a few miles down the road, I caught
up with him at a rest stop. I looked on the side of the car, and
it had "turbo" written on it. It was the turbo that made it go
so fast. In 1 Corinthians 14:4 "He who speaks in a tongue
edifies himself, but he who prophesies edifies the church."
In verse 14 it says, "If I pray in a tongue, my spirit prays." I
got the engine when I got saved. Ask Jesus for the baptism
in the Holy Spirit with the evidence of speaking in tongues
(Acts 2:4) - and you will receive the turbo for added power!

_____
_____
_____
_____
_____

December 28

Call to Me

Have you ever wondered what the Lord wants you to do, or have you been confused in what direction to go in a certain area? I'm sure all of us have experienced this one time or another. In Psalm 50:15, "Call upon Me in the day of trouble; and I will deliver thee." Have you ever thought the line was busy or you dialed the wrong number? In Psalm 145:18, it says the Lord is near when you call; don't go by feeling or circumstances. So the next time you want to call, just pick the heavenly phone up and dial F-A-I-T-H - that's FAITH. Without it – it's impossible to please Him.

_____

_____

_____

_____

_____

December 29

Tree Limb

Did you ever hear about the man who fell off the edge of a cliff, and grabbed a tree limb that was sticking out from the cliff? While he was hanging there he said, "God help me!" A voice came from heaven saying "Let go of the tree limb." He said, "Is there anybody else up there?" In Proverbs 3:5 the Bible says, "Trust in the Lord with all your heart, and lean not on your own understanding." When you are in a tight situation, trust God to help you. Don't try to figure it out on your own; believe what the Bible says about what you are going through. Stand on His Word day after day, until it comes to pass. Don't struggle hanging on the side of that cliff; let go in faith - and you will go up and not down!

_____
_____
_____
_____
_____

December 30

Not Taking for Granted

When you were growing up, did you ever take your parents for granted? We always had food in the refrigerator, it was warm in the winter time, we would always have clean clothes to wear, clean bed to sleep in. I used to take them for granted. Today I am so thankful that I had parents that loved me. In Ephesians 5:20 the Bible says, "Giving thanks always for all things to God the Father in the name of our Lord Jesus Christ." Let us thank God every day for our salvation. Let's be careful not to take it for granted. Go to your parents and friends who have sown good things in you and thank them. It is because of their prayers and love for you, that you are where you are today – let's always be thankful.

December 31

Mighty Man of Valor

Have you ever heard the devil speaking to you and saying things like, "You aren't really a Christian, look at how many times you've failed. You big phony, you can't witness - look at everybody laughing at you when you forget that scripture you wanted to remember." Have you ever felt like an unlikely candidate? In Judges 6:12 the Bible says the Angel of the Lord appeared to him, and said to him, "The Lord is with you, oh mighty man of valor!" Gideon was hiding from the enemy, I am sure he didn't feel like a mighty man of valor. Don't dwell on what the devil tells you; dwell on what God tells you. So get out there, oh mighty man and lady of valor and win some souls for Jesus!

CPSIA information can be obtained
at www.ICGtesting.com
Printed in the USA
BVOW08s0542290817
493308BV00001B/1/P